White Shorts, White Socks

DAVINDER SANGHA

DEDICATION and ACKNOWLEDGMENTS

Dedicated to all the players, officials, hanger ons
I've been involved with, who enhanced my life

Copyright © 2024 Davinder Sangha

All rights reserved.

WHITE SHORTS WHITE SOCKS

Introduction. 7

An unexpected performance - 4th August 2003. 10

Dodgy breakfasts - 16th August 2003 25

A cup for the rubbish teams - 20th August 2003 30

3-0 up within 10 minutes - 23rd August 2003. 34

Defeating superior opponents - 27th August 2003. 37

Horrible Low Fell - 3rd September 2003. 41

Harper turns on the style in 6-a-side - 4th September 2003. 46

Dixon steps in dog shit - 6th September 2003. 49

Wardle's stench prevents any man marking - 10th September 2003. 52

Racism and a last gasp equaliser - 13th September 2003. 57

Mid-life crisis fanny magnet problems - 16th September 2003. 62

Crashing back to Earth - 20th September 2003. 64

New Tango please - 27th September 2003. 68

Faith restored - 11th October 2003. 70

Faith renewed - 18th October 2003. 76

Faith comes crashing down - 25th October 2003. 79

6-1, cold feet and a runny nose - 1st November 2003. 83

Premonitions and a drop out - 8th November 2003. 85

Lack of interest - 15th November 2003. 88

Guilt of racism - 18th November 2003. 91

Point blank in the face for Kelsey - 22nd November 2003. 94

Mud caked, but victorious - 29th November 2003. 96

Running like clockwork - 6th December 2003. 99

Eleven goals down - 13th December 2003. 102

Gourlay quits - 20th December 2003. 105

New Year walloping - 10th January 2004. 109

Mountain Daisy defeat - 17th January 2004 111

WHITE SHORTS WHITE SOCKS

Team meeting - 20th January 2004. 116

A bright day, a brilliant performance - 7th February 2004 118

Defeated in the Final - 12th February 2004 121

Baker returns - 14th February 2004 125

Twigs and car parts for net pegs - 21st February 2004 130

Comfortable victory - 20th March 2004 135

A hammering - 27th March 2004 139

Tactics, tactics, tactics - 8th April 2004 142

4-4 draw - 10th April 2004 145

Daisy again - 17th April 2004 151

Dixon turns up in a suit - 21st April 2004 154

Gourlay returns - 6th May 2004 157

What's the first rule for a manager arranging a squad? 161

Quitting the League - 17th June 2004 165

The beginning of the "Lost Year" - 4th July 2004 168

Tash, bang, wallop – Part 1 - 18th July 2004 171

Searing heat - 26th July 2004 175

Humidity - 29th July 2004 178

Tash, bang, wallop – Part 2 - 5th August 2004 181

A great win, without a goalkeeper - 8th August 2004 186

Another win - 19th August 2004 189

The reason it's expensive for normal people to play football
- 22nd August 2004 191

Defeating an African XI - 26th September 2004 193

Fines owed - 26th September 2004 196

Defeating a poor league, off the pitch - 12th October 2004 198

The Police visit about a dodgy message - 14th November 2004 202

WHITE SHORTS WHITE SOCKS

It's 2024, 20 years later, and I'm still flogging a dead horse
– September 2024 204
The following pages contain articles and messages gathered
since 1999. 208
A random message on Sassco.co.uk message board
- 2nd August 2003 208
A Sunderland Earthquake, posted on 19th July 2003.
Posted By: Redhouse Reporter 213
Wayne Greenwell: Being diagnosed and treated for Cancer
– 13th February 2016 216

WHITE SHORTS WHITE SOCKS

WHITE SHORTS WHITE SOCKS

Introduction.

What happens when you have an argument with the wife, the police are called and then you get "advised" to leave the house. Well, most would grab their wallet, a decent pair of clothes and their mobile phone. I personally would do the same, but I must add to that by lugging a full set of strips, nets, corner flags and at least one match standard ball.

That was my priority, and for two years of my life (or one season 2003 to 2004) it was an attempt to bring together a genuinely diverse crew to attempt to conquer the world (or at least in and around the SR5 post code area).

Sounds normal you would think. The only difference is that I am Indian, and the team was (and still is) all white. Also, we were based in Sunderland. It seems unique and weird when you think about it, but for me it was normal and for my players it was normal as well.

WHITE SHORTS WHITE SOCKS

The diary you are about to read details that remarkable season. The first year isn't discussed much, as the diary in its present form started in the second season. I changed my writing style in the second season from the boring, "Player one passes to player two. Player three receives the ball…." To what I really thought.

Ironically, the game action is hardly mentioned, due to my opinions of the day overriding everything else. The diary was sometimes written on the day or a few days after the events, so sometimes the writing style is different. I was going to change it all to one or the other, but looking over it now, it conveys my true feelings. Sometimes, immediately pissed off, or other times more relaxed and reflective after a few days (but usually still pissed off).

On 17th of June 2004, the team named Sassco.co.uk 11-a-side officially ended its two-year stint in the diabolical Tyne & Wear League. Reasons were varying. One was the fact that the players failed to stump up some cash before a deadline I gave them and more importantly, we were to be held up on disrepute charges, which put us in limbo and are detailed near the end of this diary.

So, it's was an ideal ending point from where I can

look back on. Ironically, I'm looking back at this diary as a whole, twenty years later, with a view to creating a better formatted version for Amazon Kindle. When I first compiled it, the diary was just a section on a website. Since then, I tried to make it more independent and less localised, so anyone who wasn't aware of the area would have some semblance of understanding.

I'm now 52 years old, well into my second marriage, new job, older kids, one grandchild, and even a cat. The team started in late 1999, so we're heading into our 25th anniversary in 2025.

I look back on the comments and reports I wrote, and some are shockingly harsh. I'm surprised I never got a punch in the face for it, but it's a snapshot of the era, where swearing at someone was less of an issue in comparison to now. However, I have tempered things and removed some of the unnecessary language – out of being more mature.

The great thing for me is that the players from that early era, still pop up now and then, so the staying power is still around.

I hope you enjoy reading it and any feedback is always appreciated.

An unexpected performance - 4th August 2003.

This was it. This is where the story begins. It was the major Sassco 11-a-side encounter against a team full of overpaid and overstuffed superstars. Our team were optimistic for the forthcoming season, and with me having invested in some freeze spray and some heat spray, we had a lot to look forward to.

But so did our opposition. Durham City Reserves were unquestionably a brilliant team. Strong in every department, they beat us 8-1 in our first ever game as an 11-a-side team last year on the same pitch. The team was in a much higher (and more expensive) league. We were in what you would call the bog-standard Saturday morning or Sunday morning league.

There were differences though on this day as we had had a season of difficulties behind us.

WHITE SHORTS WHITE SOCKS

We had Billy Harper, turncoat, as co-manager on the other side. I had dragged him out of one of his many retirements, last season, to debut for us as a player and he always gave his all (as well as his famous opinions). Harper is a unique person. He has an opinion on everyone, and it usually kicks him up the arse eventually. Ironically, he is a very accomplished footballer, and I rate him very highly, but rumours still abound about his glorious footballing past. We've asked him for proof of his countless trophies, which he never stops talking about, but no one has ever seen anything about them. Also, one of his mates, while in conversation with someone let loose. Harper, making one of his many comments said something like, "in our days we'd do better than that". His mate is rumoured to have said, "Aye, Harper, but you were shite!" There was another incident when the Tash (as I tend to call him), was arrested after punching a bloke in a lay-by somewhere down south in one of his many sales journeys. The Tash has a huge physical problem. He's small, squat and well-built and used to have very clone, early 80's moustache. Now, I've read a book by a bloke called Jim Hutton, who was Freddie Mercury's boyfriend, and the Tash looks exactly like him. This guy had turned up and asked the Tash (who was munching into his sandwich) if "he'd like to go somewhere quiet…" The Tash launched into him and got arrested. When I heard about it, I thought "it could only happen to the Tash".

But before we turn to the game against Mr. Harpers superstars, I think it's better to give a brief background on the 11-a-side team itself.

I run two six-a-side leagues played at a complex based in Downhill in Sunderland. They've been running since 1999 and from these leagues, I've met some remarkable personalities and players. It was inevitable then that I'd eventually start up an 11-a-side team. Cost was always going to be the problem. I wasn't working at the time, but I had some cash earmarked from the profits for the six-a- side to pump into the team. I've never really made a great profit on the six-a-side. Much of the cash goes straight back into the leagues. I'd spent money on custom patched balls – you know the ones around in the 70's – and had them imported *en masse* from India. I conned the owner that I was running a huge multinational organisation, and he printed some off for me with the Sassco logos on. I also imported some Adidas shirts direct from Germany. I have a big problem with teams wearing horrible kits and being a graphic designer and marketeer, I'm a bit of a control freak over how things look. The Adidas shirts look fantastic and certainly put us in a different stead. "We maybe shite," I tend to say. "But at least we look good."

But despite the good background and investment (nearly a grand!!), the past 2002 to 2003 season was nothing short of miserable.

Sassco started with two friendly defeats including an 8-1 walloping off the aforementioned, Durham Reserves and we were set for a third, after being 2-0 down against a team called Hogan's. Yet we clawed it back and won 3-2. We then beat the incumbent league champs in the league we were entering, 4-1 in our last friendly before opening in the actual league itself with three wins. It all turned bad after Keith Mouat; our main defender was injured in a 3-1 victory over a team called South Shields. Keith Mouat was a definite one to look at. Probably the tallest person I've ever seen. He was used bit part by other teams, but I chose to have him as our main fulcrum in the centre half position. When playing his leg reached footballs that no other persons would even if they had a head start. I don't think I've ever seen him break sweat when (or if) he runs. Our biggest tragedy was that he was out for months and probably single handily resulted in our miserable season. We lost heavily against several teams and players dropped out and came in and so on. The morale was shocking.

WHITE SHORTS WHITE SOCKS

I nearly quit in December 2002. I had started working at the Barclays call centre after being out of work for too long in my opinion. There were no graphic design jobs available, so I went into my first call centre job. The work was monotonous, but easy money. I did manage to blag Tuesday evenings off though (it was a late shift always) to play football. Barclays thought I was looking after my son. A big problem was working on Saturdays and evenings which really put a spanner into my evening six-a-side and Saturday 11-a-side encounters. Luckily, I eventually got out in January 2003 when I started work at a biotech firm which deals with forensic and DNA testing. The 11-a-side team itself was nearly disbanded during the winter of 2002 because of my earlier work. I also owed around £100 for insurance and £120 for the pitch, and having just bought a house, was in no mood to empty my pockets.

Therein lies the problem with running a local team. Most managers are idiots and stump out the cash from their own pocket just to be popular and hopefully have some wags pat him on the back in the pub, saying, "Aye, yeev gorra cracking team marra…" I'm simply not like that. I've no interest in being popular and demand full payments from each player for each game (usually £2).

WHITE SHORTS WHITE SOCKS

Ironically, I think that's what made the Sassco team so united. The remaining players understand the way I thought and understood that it's their team. When I put it to them the amount, we needed I thought it would end there.

To my surprise, all the players chipped in large amounts of hard cash which essentially saved the team.

In return, I made an agreement that the players who'd paid the most would be permanently in the team. This hampered our chances but did create an unbreakable bond. To cap it all, we eventually managed to get a sponsor, a company called EMS Europe, which pumped hard cash into the club in return for me designing a website for them. This was enough to keep us going for at least two more seasons. We soon had a healthy bank balance in preparation for the forthcoming season.

But during the 2002 and 2003 season, we had some genuine nightmares.

One of the worst defeats was a 15-1 away hammering against Mountain Daisy. We had Sunderland AFC's youth trainer, Ed Cook, who also played, on and off, in the six-a-side leagues, giving us a 15-minute warm up which completely knackered us. We were literally blowing out of our arses when the ref kicked off the game.

One of our earlier games, we had a memorable encounter against the International Cultural Centre, a team made up of asylum seekers. We were returning after our first defeat away to Low Fell, who were based in Gateshead (therefore are hated Geordies, scum, scabs, etc.) and presented a much-changed team. We won 15-3, but the funniest thing was a full-scale fight between the Arabic members of the ICC. The craziest thing is that I was accused of racism after the game, and it went to a tribunal. I retorted with a strong abusive letter which scared the committee off. I've dubbed the committee as "death row" due to their age. The committee was a genial bunch of aging gentlemen and "yes" men, with one woman on board. But with my experience of running a modern, internet aware league, their ideas were backwards. The retiring league secretary, Alan Young, still spent a year and a day typing out league tables and results and rules on a rickety typewriter, while I made sure the full name of our team was Sassco.co.uk, due to people searching for it on the Internet.

We also lost humiliatingly against teams like the "The Club". Both games against them, we should have got something. But their over aggressiveness put us off. The

WHITE SHORTS WHITE SOCKS

Club are full of strong and aggressive footballers who enjoy their fair share of crunching tackles. We did manage to grab the highly rated "Corby" out of his semiretirement to play for us. But I ditched him when he did not pay his subs. Corby, also known as Anthony Richardson, was supposed to be a key member of the team and was there when we turned a 2-0 deficit in a preseason game against Hogan's into a 3-2 win. Corby has been known to me for years and used to play in my Sassco.co.uk team in the only time we won a trophy. He tends to complain that he's getting old but has been saying that since 1991.

At the end, we kept on losing and despite this; we still managed to get a good turnout. For the last game of the 2002-2003 season, I severely put my foot down and demanded that everyone be there. And they turned up in their droves. We had a full squad of around fifteen to choose from.

I made some much-criticised changes. In came Steve Stubbs in central defence. Stubba is nothing more than a leech. He barely pays his subs and bums money off everyone. In the football side of things, his earlier positions were usually on the flanks or in the full back positions. I also put the returning Mickey Pearson in central midfield and the ageing Harper in attack.

WHITE SHORTS WHITE SOCKS

Pearson was a key member at the start of the season, but work commitments forced him out. He is a decent player, but Harper seems to think that he has the potential of God. I tend to disagree. Pearson's had some decent games but never shone. But then again, he is a young lad and needs to decide on a position to keep hold of. I also told Jon Wardle to fuck off to the Club, as he was increasingly complaining about decisions. Jon has always been our shining light. Although I'm convinced his name was spelt wrong on his birth certificate because his parents couldn't spell. Looking at him, you'd think he's just some other fat roofer, who plays Sunday morning football. He's overweight and looks like his suffering from asthma. But behind the freakish outlook, he had frightening pace and a lethal shot. He was my captain and did have a right to make his comments known. But my decision stood. He is by far our most dangerous attacker, with his ample weight deceiving the opposition in masking his pace and ability. I put him up front as opposed to midfield, which is where he wanted to play. Despite conceding an early goal, we eventually won 2-1 with goals from Harper and Wardle.

Yes, we did it. Sassco finally won a game in style. Up against the New Derby, we had a full squad to choose from. It started with a bit of controversy, with Jon

WHITE SHORTS WHITE SOCKS

Wardle complaining bitterly about Steve Stubbs being place in defence. I also put two attacking wingers on the full back positions. Wayne Galey came in late in the season. He's a quiet lad but seems quite cool when on the ball. Dave Gourlay on the other hand tends to think he's God's gift and widely regarded as one of the most hated players in the region. Physically he looks like Gerd Muller (although I'm sure he's not an alcoholic). I really don't know where this hatred of him comes from. Personally, I get on well with him and rate his skills highly. Football wise, his nonaggressive style isn't really suited for attacking positions in the team, so I decided to place him as a full back.

It started very promisingly with every player battling to the max to win the ball in midfield and break up the play. But unfortunately, New Derby opening the scoring. Jon Wardle had a truly glorious chance to equalise moments later, but his shot just squeezed wide. It was after this when Muer's picked out Harper with a pinpoint pass to tie the game at 1-1.

Now Muers is a true enigma. Tall and strong but sometimes plays truly shite. He's also going bald as well so shaves his head. People still call him a "ginger" (He is also known as Dunston, the orangutan from "Dunston Checks In") though. So, it was quite ironic that he set up Harper, one of his main critics. "Couldn't kick shit off a step," was one of the Tash's comments on Muers.

A truly outstanding central defensive performance from Stubbs was the highlight of the game. Not a single challenge was shirked as the defence remained firm.

Galey was outstanding and Greenwell, another regular grabbed from the 6-a-side, was truly awesome and spent most of the game winning the ball back from almost impossible situations.

The second saw my policy of making substitutions continue, with Chris Dixon replacing Mark Kelsey. Now there's two contrasting people. Dixon is known as the iceman. Tall and pacey and it seems when Dixon scores a goal, he isn't happy about it. I'm sure when he wins the lottery, he'll have the same face on. Kelsey's is truly shocking. With several teeth missing, his mouth resembles one of our defensive walls – plenty of gaps, but he's a proper terrier as well and has had his fair share of sending offs. With his mate, David Leithes (Leithy aka Alfie – a cross between Shane Ritchie and Bill Tarmy), they tend to go to South Shields on a Friday night to pick up some fat lasses.

I also brought on Dave Gourlay and took Harper off. Harper was blowing out of his arse currently. Both changes were much to the chagrin of Wardle. I explained my decisions to Wardle by telling him to "Fuck off you fat cunt. Get on with it". In the second half, instantly Dixon had a chance which he would normally put away. But coming back from injury, a weak foot allowed the opposition to win the ball. The majority of the second half saw New Derby pounding against us, and normally you would have expected them to score, but it wasn't to be and eventually New Derby faded away, half expecting a draw. In one of these late attacks, Dave Gourlay took control of the ball in an awkward situation and launched it towards Wardle, who made no mistake to make it 2-1 with ten minutes to go. Mark Muers, who had a truly brilliant game, hobbled off to be replaced by Anthony Mouat. Now there is a sight. Anth is the brother of Keith Mouat, and personally, I blame the milk man, because they don't look alike. Anth is huge and wide, but he instantly made his mark on the game. His first move was literally pole axing one of the opposition. To cries of "he's killed him, he's killed him!" he rolled over and said (after the game) that he bit his own tongue in the process. He also helped by using his vast frame to avert a late and almost certain goal.

In the changing room afterwards, I let rip on Wardle, with a torrent of "I told you so" inspired abuse. I also had to keep Stubbs in check as his boxer's good looks were expanding his head with his man of the match performance. "Stubba", as centre half, was a truly outstanding player on the day, and even surprised me. Before the game, Wardle had complained that Stubba couldn't handle the defence. I told him that I needed his aggressive and terrier like persistence. My reasoning paid off as we won in the end, down to Stubba's performance. So, the philosophy is that I am more aware of a players ideal position then the player himself. Gourlay wants to be a player behind the front two (in the hole), Wardle wants to be a centre midfielder and Stubba wants to be the next Pope – but they're all not ideal roles for them.

The team was also bolstered for the forthcoming season with Mark Baker joining on the recommendation of Wayne Greenwell. Neil Maven and James Dickinson also came in having signed last season, but never really called upon. Baker is an outstanding player, but his attitude is sometimes strange. I think he has a real problem with authority which would rear its head later on in the season. But at the moment, he was the man to fill in for midfield as Pearson didn't seem too interested in re-joining the team. Neil Maven was just the type of person we needed. A tough tackling, high aggressive centre half. We'd played against him when he played for Hogan's the season before. James Dickinson was nothing short of Brilliant. Jiff, as he's known, has some searing pace which caught out every team we played against.

The team I put out for the pre-season friendly against Durham, was on the similar lines and shape to our last league game. Replacing the Tash, who was now on the other side as Manager, was Dixon and Mark Baker, as mentioned came in for Pearson. We kicked off and matched them for the opening salvo. Unfortunately, we couldn't deal with a Si Williamson throw in. Si was a tall gangling player who was very skilful and blessed with an outstanding throw – he also worked at the complex itself. This throw resulted in a goal, but the floodgates didn't open. Their backline was overly arrogant and one of our superstars, Staples stole the ball off them to miss a sitter. Staples isn't even the size of a decent shit, but he's got this uncanny ability of being our best winner of the ball – in the air! His aggression in winning the ball back is also a huge boost. He is a genuine terrier like tackler and is probably just about the same size. I once washed a shirt in 60 degrees just to reduce it in size for him to wear. Luckily the opposition didn't learn, and their back line again lost the ball. Wardle stole in managed to equalise. We were clearly matching them man for man. We had another of our ex's (thank God), Anth Mouat on the opposite line giving us grief, but as always, we responded in kind.

Muers for once turned the abuse that they (and I) gave to him and easily danced past his marker. They were becoming scared as arguments broke out between them.

The second half saw the introduction of our two new lads. Neil Maven and Jiff, who made an instant impact with a stunning response to an equally stunning goal from their team. It was 2-2 currently and we clearly were more likely to score. But opportunities were squandered, and we did not deal with a cross, again, for them to go 3-2 ahead. At the death, Dixon missed a sitter, and their keeper pulled off a stunning save from Muers. The opposition were shell shocked. Harper shook my hand congratulating me on the performance. It wasn't what they expected and the vast number of supporters they had saw our potential. Keith Mouat was on as a second half sub for them, and halfway during the game had the cheek to ask me when "our" first game was! We responded in cries of "turncoat". Muers turned both Keith and the rest of his defence inside out, and it got to a stage when they are doubling up on him. Christ! Doubling up on Muers! They gave him more respect than I ever did. For us, Stubba had another remarkable game in defence. He won everything set at him and was comfortable in the role. I clearly remember people telling me about his performance against New Derby was a one-off. Eat your words chaps.

WHITE SHORTS WHITE SOCKS

Dodgy breakfasts - 16th August 2003

Our preparation for our first 11-a-side encounter against Studio 2000 hardly went to plan. Firstly, I came down with a horrendous fever late in the night and had around three hours sleep. So, apologies if this write up is a bit wobbly. In the morning, I woke up at around 5pm and went ahead to shit and piss through every available orifice. Must have been the Mexican chicken sandwich I got from Bakers Oven on Friday.

I struggled to get to the complex but got there in reasonable time. The team scheduled to turn up for 9:45am turned up on time, apart from Boothy, Wardle and Stubba. Boothy is my righthand man for the team. A shy, accountant, number cruncher type person. We worked together before I got the boot at his workplace, but the footballing relationship just blossomed. Boothy handles all the cash side of things while I control the team itself. He also does a lot of the running about by

WHITE SHORTS WHITE SOCKS

picking up the likes of Wardle and co who lived on the South side of the river.

This time, though, Wardle decided he wanted a bacon and egg sandwich, so they were delayed. Another problem: when putting the nets on, all the fools bent all the pegs by hammering them too hard. It's safe to say the nets weren't put up as per FIFA standard, but it beats the usual range of car parts we used to use last season when the pegs ran out. The team we had was quite good. Dave Gourlay, having checked the William Harper Book of Football Injuries decided he had a foot or leg injury and bottled it. Muers was missing and when the celebrations died down the team was as follows: Watson in goal. Stubbs, Maven centre halves with Galey and Booth full backs. I put Dickinson on the right and Staples on the left. Greenwell and Baker in centre midfield. Dixon and Wardle were in attack. Now I haven't mentioned Watson. He's a truly outstanding keeper and still wears the multicoloured Adidas shirt he used to wear in the late 80's. Not a big person, quite fat now, but, by God, he doesn't half jump around, quite unlike a fat lad.

The game was one I expected to win. But it was against the same team with which we had two entertaining 3-3 draws last season and it was all down to

WHITE SHORTS WHITE SOCKS

defensive mistakes. This time it was completely different. Stubba and Mav were outstanding in defence and responded to everything set to them. We were half decent on defending corners as well. The problem was up front. Firstly, we were getting caught offside too easily. So excruciatingly frustrating because our front line is probably one of the fastest in the league. We did eventually open the scoring after Dixon, for once onside, beat his man and despite a tussle, managed to let loose an unstoppable shot to make it 1-0. Unfortunately, Studio equalised from a penalty after Stubba's Neanderthal arms, more used to climbing trees, hit the ball in the penalty area. After this, Greenwell nearly scored from a corner kick and Stubba himself bought off a fantastic save from the opposition keeper. Boothy seemed to cope well with his left back position despite being right footed. One thing we all noticed from the game was how fat Boothy's arse was. The best way to describe it would be KFC drumsticks with extra batter on. Now, as most people know, because I tell them all the time, the shorts we wear are Adidas imports from Germany. The sizes are comfortable, and everyone seems okay in them. Apart from Boothy who looks like he was poured into them. Every time he got the ball it was to a synchronised chorus of "I see you baby…shaking that ass." Poor lad.

WHITE SHORTS WHITE SOCKS

Anyway, it was 1-1 at the half time stage. My team talk was basic, but I told the lads that getting caught offside once or twice was okay, but ten times made them look like dick heads. In the second half we went ahead again with a stunning Dickinson goal, but eventually the opposition equalised, and it was 2-2.

The final minutes showed a bit of disorganisation. Dixon, who switched with Dickinson on the wing, was completely out of position on most occasions – either that or he was doing his Johan Cruyff impression. Wardle didn't do much apart from one decent shot and a few minutes arguing with the referee. Overall, our captain was disappointing.

Our main strength is our captain's abilities to score from almost any distance, but we never take advantage of it. So many missed opportunities. I was well pissed off. Staples got the ball stuck under his foot a few times when a clear chance was on. Also, there was too much needless passing in the last third when a shot should have been on.

The crowd we had was quite decent. Harper turned up with his new streamlined haircut. Obviously, an offshoot of the Atkins Diet he was on after Dixon tore him a new arsehole in the six-a-side, earlier in the month. Kelsey was also there along with Anth Mouat.

WHITE SHORTS WHITE SOCKS

Corby made a welcome return watching on the sidelines and he was much impressed with the performance. Corby's opinion is probably the one which I always take on board and to be perfectly honest, I was very impressed as well. The team seemed much more stable. Last season we went all to pot when Keith Mouat got injured, which left Boothy as the only main centre half for the whole season. This time we had Stubba and Mav in that position and both did more than was expected of them. Up front we still got caught out in the offside position easily, and Wardle didn't take shots when he should have done. The reason why he didn't was because he got stuck in midfield too often. Jon is simply a shite midfielder and will always be classed as that. But he is an outstanding striker, probably one of the best in the league and when he learns to let Greenwell, Baker and co. to win the ball for him, he will shine – but only as an attacker. Greenwell is probably our best player overall. Exceptionally fit and active and quietly aggressive. A good knowledgeable player in the centre of the park – face is a bit rough though.

WHITE SHORTS WHITE SOCKS

A cup for the rubbish teams - 20th August 2003

We had a second game against Studio, but this time it was in the "mingers cup". Basically, it was a competition for the bottom few teams in the league from the previous season, and we were one of them. I put out an almost identical team, with only Muers starting as Dixon was late. Again, pre match preparations didn't really go to plan. Pearson was unavailable, Jif and Mav were both late, which meant my arse was going like the clappers, as I was expected to play.

Whenever we struggle to organise a team, my idea of the result and the match goes completely out of the window and all I want is to get 11 players on the pitch. I tried to get Keith Mouat to fill in, but he hadn't bought any kit. But lo and behold, like an image out of Lawrence of Arabia, both Jif and Mav appeared over the horizon to be able to play. Dixon eventually turned up after kick off and interpreted my "take your time." comment as sarcasm. I was serious as we had finally had 11 players and Dixon was to be a second half sub.

With a typical goalkeeper's attention span, halfway through the first half, Watson shouted out to get Dixon on - he thought we were playing with 10. Typical goalkeeper, who himself didn't have his most assured game as he spent certain moments flapping around like an injured duck.

Disappointingly we conceded off an early Studio attack. Stubbs, who was at fault for one of their goals in our league encounter, was "taken out" by a sniper on the hill, and while he was chewing the grass, they scored. We immediately took the game by the scruff of the neck and drove forward in numbers. Wayne Galey, one of our few decent players on the night, broke their offside trap to equalise and Jiff leapt twice as high as their keeper to put us 2-1 ahead. Their keeper was decidedly shaky, but we couldn't take advantage. Countless times we pierced the offside trap only to be hauled back by the referee. Sometimes we were correct, but most times we were off. It was on another of these offside occasions when Wardle broke through and slotted home.

WHITE SHORTS WHITE SOCKS

Again, like the previous game, we had too many opportunities. Staples sent me a text message prior to the game saying that he was going to get a hat-trick and perform out his skin after his below par performance last time. Lying little shit. He had around three or four shots - if I can call them shots. They were basically pass backs to their keeper. Muers missed countless chances, although they were on target and tested the keeper. Late on I began to swear heavily at Muers for no reason at all. I eventually ran out of expletives and just spent 15 minutes saying, "run you bald bastard". The reason for my discomfort was Studio's goals in the second half. It was 3-2. I had substituted Wardle at half time purely because of his lack of positional sense and we were probably worse off for it. In the first half he was defending a throw in near our corner flag. Like I said before, Jon's an excellent striker, but a truly shite midfielder and defender. Dixon replaced him and didn't fare much better. One good opportunity he had was passed to Muers, who was offside. Both teams seemed to be able to create chances from every attack, but it was Studio who seemed likely to equalise and take the game to extra time. Wardle, standing on the side-lines, made a tactical change (with my approval of course). Jiff dropped to left back, pushing Boothy to centre half. Mav moved to midfield pushing Greenwell up front. I was positive about everything apart from Greenwell up front. Greenwell himself also complained about it, but for once, things got better. Mav and Baker got a grip of midfield and we soon created some excellent chances made by winning our own ball from goal kicks.

Time eventually ran out and we were through to the Semi Final against Ivy House. Disappointing performance, which was far worse than the previous game against these. But the result was positive, and that's all that matters.

WHITE SHORTS WHITE SOCKS

3-0 up within 10 minutes - 23rd August 2003.

The best we've done to date, without any shadow of a doubt (I sound like Ray Clemence). I clearly remember the last away game against Hollymere. We had a bit part team and I turned up late after having to pick up Muers and Staples. We lost 5-4 and we were 5-1 down at one stage. Overall Hollymere destroyed us. Watson got man of the match for making some truly astounding saves.

My team talk was the usual basics. I warned them not to give corners away and needed someone to stick to the goal kicks. Galey was obvious choice, but before that, the usual organisational problems occurred. The referee didn't turn up, so we mutually decided to let Anth Mouat referee and he did a genuine and transparent job.

Amazingly we were 3-0 up within 10 minutes. Dixon, Dickinson and Wardle were on the score sheet. Dixon truly had a blinder and ended the game with a hat-trick.

I've never seen him perform to that level before. He won almost every tackle he went in for and beat the offside trap without a problem. His pace and power were causing no end of problems for the opposition. When the front men lost the ball, it was Dixon who was chasing back and doubling up to win it back. He fully deserved his hat-trick and it's been long awaited but much more welcome for his performance. All our team was completely surprised and taken aback and playing like that, it'll be hard to dislodge him. Wardle also had a fantastic game. His three goals were perfectly taken and superb for confidence. Jiff also weighed in with two strikes. The pace up front was frightening, and in contrast the defence were almost lock tight. Problems at left back though, where Boothy seems to have forgotten how to defend. His lack of left foot is a hindrance, but nevertheless he is there to do what he used to do in the central position – which is defend. Galey was phenomenal. From his perfect goal kicks to his excellent setup play. He combined well with Baker and Greenwell in a truly brilliant performance. Jiff, at one staged looked like he received a bad injury as he lay prostrate on the floor. People were shouting for water and the magic sponge, but having the team spirit we had, none of our players were asking for the water for Jiff.

WHITE SHORTS WHITE SOCKS

Nevertheless, Jiff being a Southwick boy could, no doubt, dig a hole in the ground and discover water with no problems. One black spot was Stubba getting a yellow card like the nonce he is. He won a ball while on the ground and sent Wardle through. But some afters made the referee (who had turned up after 11 minutes) stop play and award a free kick. It seems as if Ocean Finance will be getting a call as Stubba is way back with his subs payments and now has a lovely Durham FA £7 fine to pay.

Hollymere at one stage in the first half clawed it back to 3-2. Muers at the time lost the ball and fell flat on his arse. While we were pissing ourselves laughing, they scored the goal. We weren't wobbling though. Wardle soon hit back to make it 4-2. In the second half it was all us. I made a like for like substitution by taking Muers off and putting Staples on. It made an immediate impact. Staples lost the ball and they scored. Well done little fella. Still though, we were too good. Wayne Greenwell had three long shots which were way off, and Dixon missed a sitter at the end. But all in all, a tremendous performance. The cliché is that "we'll hammer a team one day…" and we did today. All my anxiety and frustration after the last two games was gone. Both my strikers gained hat-tricks and the team was excellent. No complaints. Well done lads.

Defeating superior opponents - 27th August 2003.

I'm not a huge fan of the Sandhill's. Firstly, they are the double winners and secondly, I suffered my only form of racial abuse at their pitch last season. We lost 7-1 away and I seem to remember jumping up for a ball and I'm sure (not 100% though) that the opposition player said, "Black Cunt." when he jumped with me. Never mind it wasn't obvious though. If it was, I'd be sent off as I would have studded him in the face (no I wouldn't).

But for the encounter this time, it was difficult to describe my feelings before the game. I was quietly confident, but really wasn't sure how we were going to perform. Playing against the likes of Studio and Hollymere, proved that we could beat teams which were obviously man for man, weaker than us. Last season, I could put out a supremely talented team, only to see them fail to gel and lose against inferior opposition. Mainly because of my dithering over positions. This season just felt different. I made players stick to a position. Prime example is Boothy at left back for the moment. Galey would be comfortable there, but why move Galey from right back to left back just to make Boothy more comfortable. What I'd have then is Galey playing average and Boothy playing average. What's happening now is that Galey is having a blinder each game and Boothy never looked more comfortable playing as a left back. For the whole team though, when we needed to up a gear, we did it. And against Sandhill's, we certainly shocked any independent viewer. Billy Harper asked me before the game, as I was mooching around in the Durham Reserves changing room, what I expected. I couldn't answer as I really didn't know. He then asked what I expected if the team plays to its best, and I responded that, "We'd beat them easily."

And we did.

The team was changed only slightly. Dave Robason turned up with Jon Wardle as Stubba was missing. Stubba's big problem is money. The fool always struggles to pay his subs and spends his time bumming cash off other people. He also owes £7 for his yellow

WHITE SHORTS WHITE SOCKS

card against Hollymere. Well anyway, Robason was my prime defender for last season, but selfishly decided to work on Saturday mornings for cash in hand instead of turning up week in week out to be humiliated (and to pay for it). Tall, strong and most of all, calm.

Muers was on the bench and Staples replaced him on the flanks. I was extremely close to completely ditching Muers from the team (and still am) after his attitude at being dropped. Face facts - Muers isn't really a good enough player for us this season. His work rate is almost non-existent in that we must prompt him to close players down when we don't have the ball. Also, the rest of the team have reached a higher limit in their play.

Muers best performance to date was when we beat New Derby at the end of last season. He needs to pick up that form to succeed in this team, otherwise he will be constantly subbed. Dixon was on a similar level until he obliterated his "myth" by torturing Hollymere. Muers needs a similar performance.

Sandhills seemed to be a bit arrogant in my opinion. But being League Champs and Cup Winners, you can't really blame them. They walloped us three times last season with heavy score lines. But this was completely different. We went 2-0 ahead in a quiet first half. Wardle put us 1-0 ahead and Sandhills probably expected that just to be a blip. But for them it was the beginning of a nightmare. Dixon latched on to a terrible goal kick (from their keeper, not Watty, as you'd expect) and put us 2-0 ahead. Panic stations for Sandhills. We should have been 3-0 ahead, but Wardle's goal was judged offside by the dithering referee, despite our Captain being clearly onside by running from deep.

The second half saw Muers replace Staples and a spell of bad defending for us. We simply couldn't clear the ball, and when we did, it was coming straight back. Baker had one of his weaker games. Not with his positive play, but rather when he lost the ball. Unlike the rest of the team, Baker does not chase down his own lost ball to make their players panic. Sandhills eventually scored from a dubious corner kick. The ball wasn't supposed to have crossed the line, but the referee gave it. But they deserved it as we were under intense pressure. Now if this happened last season, Sandhill's would have gone on to win. We weathered the storm and slowly built up on our first half performance. Greenwell, not our most renowned goal scorer, let loose a stunning shot after the team won the ball back, which went curling into the back of the net. It was around 25 yards out and it was game over for Sandhills. We were toying with them now. Jiff put us 4-1 ahead to humiliate them and to top it off, Muers grabbed the fifth and final goal after his original shot was saved by the goalkeeper. He nodded the return into the back of the net.

So, the moral of this story is that Sassco are far superior to I expected them to be. The work rate is simply stunning. The long balls sent by Sandhills were expertly dealt with by Galey, Mav, Roba and Boothy. It was hard work dealing with all the high balls, but we did it. We gave more than the number of corners away I wanted to, but they only scored their dubious goal from one.

WHITE SHORTS WHITE SOCKS

Horrible Low Fell - 3rd September 2003.

Ahh, Low Fell! What wonderful memories this place conjures up. A virtual oasis within the seething (some would call mingin) metropolis known as Gateshead. The Low Fell pitch is at Kibblesworth (yes, you work it out). We struggled through the control checkpoint as most of us were foreigners in a strange land. Apart from Stubba, of course. He fit in perfectly with the natives. And more to the point, he turned up with legal tender in his pocket.

A £2 dint in his £18 debt. It seems I won't have to instigate a CCJ form him after all.

For the game itself, we were playing the dreaded Geordies from Gatesheeed, but personally I have had bad memories from visiting Geordie land. My first memory as a young child was with an earlier 11-a- side when we turned up in Season 2001-2002 and saw our game cancelled due to some drinking on the side of the pitch.

Lo and behold, the referee didn't even give us the opportunity to warn them off. Conspiracy theories ranged from the committees ambition to remove the team from the League, to a communist plot arranged by the fat bloke down the pub. Eventually it all got sorted out later, with my old team, Toddy's, in the clear and DFA questioning the reasons for completely cancelling the game. My other pubescent memories are of the Season 2002-2003. The wonderful day when we turned up with God knows how many new players and got a Geordie Geronimo with an 8-1 thrashing. I remember because I was ill at the time, had an argument with the "Tash", who nearly walked off, and spent the game watching poor Alfie Leithes meandering in the forward position. Boothy was the only survivor from that catastrophe which set us on our miserable season, last season.

Anyway, enough of the reminisces and back to the new and improved formula called the Sassco Warriors. A few weeks back, I would have been unsure of this result, but now a win was paramount. We had performed to a level which was expected but had surprised a lot of independent commentators (and the "Tash"). I was nervous. We had to give respect, but we didn't. For the first half, we had more chance of clearing one of Stubba's cheques than the ball itself. We were disjointed and looked uncomfortable. Lucky for us that the scum were so bad in the last third that we didn't go a goal down. They even failed to take advantage of the corners we, again, gave away. I even saw Mav threatening to walk off the pitch after I ranted at him kicking thin air instead of a ball. It wasn't really directed at him, but it was a general thing, and changes had to be made. (plus, I shit myself in case he decided to chin me).

At half time the ineffective Baker was subbed and amazingly, Muers remained on the pitch. He did well in the first and for once I spent most of the time congratulating him instead of saying, "run, you bald bastard, run!" Eventually we calmed down and scored an opener from a very narrow angle. It was 1-0 and the result really wasn't in doubt, despite some scares which were made by us. Stubba had come on at half time to restore some order and despite jumping around (and looking) like an orangutan, he played well. Galey had a weak game and lost the ball too easily in dangerous positions, but we had the ever reliably Robason in as centre half. Boothy also sometimes did not clear when he had the chance. But then when your arse is a fat as Boothy's and the fact that you pivot like a battleship evens things out.

WHITE SHORTS WHITE SOCKS

An eventual second goal game from Greenwell and out popped the thong that Staples had got off some dirty slapper. Personally, I think he buys them himself as they look his size. Dirty little shit. He came on himself to replace Dixon, who was back to his old ways, by missing three quality chances. But I can't really blame him. The whole team was off key. We did score a third and it was Fatty Wardle, who was receiving significant racial abuse from some illegitimate children on the sidelines. He threatened to either kick the shit out or adopt a few of them. Problem with Jon was that he'd come straight from work and looked like a right minger. He claims he's a roofer, but when Robason and Dixon turn up in a suit and tie alongside him, I reckon he's just a big sack of sweaty shite and looks that way normally. He took his goal well, though and we did get a fourth and final goal. Watson made some good saves near the end and his counterpart, Baz, for Low Fell did extremely well himself, considering he isn't their standard 'keeper. But the result was good in the end, and we'll look back on it in reflection to the fact that we can't simply turn up and expect teams to roll over just because we are actually half decent this season. Hard work and perseverance held out in the end. I still think we would have won had we gone a goal down, but all in all, revenge is so sweet. But this was only a cup game. I

WHITE SHORTS WHITE SOCKS

don't know – how many cups?

Fixture back log anyone?

Harper turns on the style in 6-a-side - 4th September 2003.

A sad note before I continue. We discovered that Mark Baker's mother had passed away after a long battle with cancer. Mark was playing against Low Fell and like a lot of people do when dealing with grief, it's better to get on with life and enjoy the things such as football to keep you going. It's not connected, but when I had problems, the football kept me going strong.

Back to the football, for me, as organiser of the six-a-side league, I must stay until the very end. Which basically means sitting frozen watching two miserable teams playing each other in front of a crowd of around two people (including me). Most of the action takes place on the other side of the fence, where David "Alfie" Leithes usually brings a mini barbecue and starts rustling up some salmonella burgers and Cheesey Ross, another local stalwart, slowly drifts away into never-

never land after raising his drug intake during the course of the night.

Tonight, was special though. The main event was the fact that Harper made a secret and surprise return to six-a-side football. He had signed on for the hapless and bottom team, O'Neill Sports. Mr. Harper – what can we say about him. Harper was the manager of Toddy's for around three long seasons before quitting in disgust and then wanting to come back. His problem was that none of the players wanted him back. An (according to himself) excellent footballing mind, but his body simply wasn't designed to cope with his knowledge. Harper had, on and off, played in the six-a-side league on a regular basis. He played a major role in my original six-a- side team, but injuries sent him into retirement.

Tonight, he was playing for O'Neill Sports. The team had won jack shit since day one and were always struggling. They were playing against one of Harper's ex-teams and the rivalry was immense. For the first time in ages, we had a huge crowd, and they saw a classic.

Harper's boys went 2-0 ahead amidst the "Tash" making his comments known and looking absolutely ridiculous in his green and white top and running shorts and basketball boots. But the other clawed it back and it seemed as if they would win. But lo and behold, the

WHITE SHORTS WHITE SOCKS

Tash came steaming in near the end to lash in the winner and O'Neill's first points of the season.

WHITE SHORTS WHITE SOCKS

Dixon steps in dog shit - 6th September 2003.

For the record, my pre-match meal consisted of sausage, pancakes and syrup, with two hash browns (one of them Wardle's) and tea with two sugars and milk. While in McDonalds we heard that Stubba was dancing with Neil Middlemiss last night. You couldn't really think of two more contrasting personalities. Stubba with his, what shall we say? Rugged looks. Neil Middlemiss on the other hand is a dark-haired version of tin-tin and also widely regarded as one of the most hated persons in football. But looking at it from the wider picture, I think Neil is attracted by Stubba being the brute he is and Stubba attracted by Neil's boyish good looks – no guesses who's the bitch in that relationship. Also, Muers announced that he'd broken his wrist. But like most things Muer's says to people, no one gives a shit. He didn't even inform me, and it was lucky that Spice Boy Pearson and Dave Gourlay were available. Baker was also available and to be honest we had a strong team, despite Galey and Robason missing. Last season, we played the Ivy away with 10 men and won 3-1. For the new and improved Sassco team, coming back off the 4-0 away to the stench, we were highly confident. We are due to play the Ivy at home in the minger's semi-final this coming Wednesday and I was actually going to put out a team that was available on Wednesday. Staples and Muers would be on the flanks and Jiff up front with Wardle. Muer's with his broken wrist was unavailable so it was as the norm. Dixon and Wardle up front, with Jiff and Staples on the flanks. Pearson slotted in as right back in Galey's absence and Gourlay was on the bench. It was obvious that Gourlay would come on in the second half, but by then the game was over. Jiff scored both goals in the first half as we looked extremely comfortable if not a little overconfident. Team talk consisted of avoiding giving away corners and tackling (or fouling) the opposition further up the field. As expected, we gave away too many corners and the odd stupid free kick.

Second half saw Wardle fire one in and Jiff vainly trying to get his hat-trick. In the first half he hit the cross bar with an overhead kick and had a few decent chances. In the second half when in on goal, his legs gave away, or the sniper was following us around – no one's sure. At the end, Stubba who had put in two good performances back to back and another £2 towards his debt, headered in a goal which hit the cross bar and bounced back in off the 'keeper. Stubba with his mongoloid looks meandered back into his defensive position and one could not help to be reminded of all those gorilla programs on the discovery channel. Dixon had an eventful game. It started with him ripping the crust off some dog shit and accumulating a large dollop of it on his boot. It'll take more than a knife and fork to dig out the remnants between his blades. Obviously shocked and distressed by the unwelcome weight on his foot, he hit the cross bar twice but struggled to finish all game.

But the difference this season is that when a player isn't performing to his maximum, he sets options up for the teams. Countless times did Dixon set up chances for Jiff and Wardle. Eventually the remnants must have scraped away in the damp grass, but it's clear Dixon needs to compose himself on the ball and then try and find a decent pair of tweezers to pick at his boots. Staples also had a good game by setting up two goals. On several occasions, he easily out jumped his much taller counterparts to win the ball. Gourlay also settled in well after his first game since the Durham friendly, unfortunately he is missing for Wednesday. Greenwell and Baker both had uneventful but positive games. Watson performed very well in goal. He commanded his area and had a keen eye on any danger spots, by running out and grabbing or kicking the ball clear. Surprising really, it seems as if he's been poured into his kit or alternatively it's been painted on him. One bad note was that a lot of the lads didn't pay any subs. This is criminal, firstly because it tars everyone with same brush as Stubba, and secondly, we don't want to return to the situation we were in last season. Sort it out boys!

Wardle's stench prevents any man marking - 10th September 2003.

The big day. Our Semi Final against the Ivy. I expected nothing more than a win and eventually got one which was just has handsome as the last two. But coming off the back of a good performance, the team did not kick start in the first half. The team was reasonably solid.

A gamble in playing Mickey Pearson up front didn't really pay off, but the whole team was flat in the first half.

Too much overconfidence, I reckon. We weren't really in any danger, but a daft goal conceded would have made me paranoid. Robason returned for his usual midweek canter and had a good game. Stubba also made head way in reducing his debt which probably stands at around £12 now. And most surprisingly of all, Muers rang up and said he'd sawed his cast off, from a broken wrist, and was ready to play. But then the whinging began as he expected to start. Stubba was also benched in favour of Mav and Roba. I confronted everyone about late payments, and we got a good response. Boothy's the accountant and I'm the debt collector. Everyone paid up, but the fact that it was a semi-final meant we had to get linesman. One of them came from Newcastle and we had to pay his expenses. Totally ridiculous considering that Keith Brazier, our regular referee for the six-a-side leagues turned up to watch. This is unacceptable and we will be bringing it up with the organisers. It's a very expensive business running a team, so any added and unnecessary costs aren't needed. But going back to the game itself, being on a Wednesday and being the final game in our midweek series, meant we had our biggest crowd to date. The Sassco gospel is spreading, and thankfully we completed the game with a good score line.

The first half, as mentioned wasn't too good. Wardle, our inspirational captain turned up smelling rank and putrid. The kit he wore was also unwashed, and a late clash of heads in the second half meant his poor victim, not only got a headache, but also got Wardle's nits – so a shaven head then. Boothy had a contrasting game, he still forgets his left leg isn't just for bouncing someone else's baby on but can be used to trap the ball and direct it. You see Boothy got involved with a bird with two kids. It gets worse. The girl's boyfriend played in his six-a-side team. It gets even worse. He eventually left her due to hassle and she started stalking him and doing his car in. The perpetrators eventually got caught, but we had a good laugh at his expense when it was happening. Boothy's forward play (or was it foreplay) was excellent, though. He should have let loose with a shot when he was clear, which (if correct) would have flown in. Poor lad came off in the second half for Stubba. But I got a text from him later that night with him whinging about being subbed or being criticised. I didn't hold back in the reply. I told him to not bother turning up on Saturday and go on the piss with Muers, another one of our whingers. The reply was grovelling to say the least. That's the difference this season – no pissing about. If a player isn't happy, he can fuck off and be miserable somewhere else. The likes of Muers and Booth are clearly inferior to the likes of Jiff, Staples and Gourlay who all take up their positions.

Stubba was on the bench and didn't really complain much. The aggressive features of our "new" star soon shone through as he looked comfortable when he came on. Ten minutes into the second half I made another change. Pearson was subbed for Muers. Now Pearson had an average game, but like I said before, the whole team didn't really fire on all cylinders. But then poxy Muers – he who shaves his head because everyone calls him a "ginger bastard" and the fact that he is going bald. He did okay as he'd come on and we scored not too long after when the confidence was high. He missed a glorious chance which raised a huge cheer – probably the loudest of the night. Luckily, we were 2-0 up at the time. Wardle had opened our scoring. A loose ball dropped to the Fatty, and he lashed it in, upsetting the goal pegs in the process. It was over for the Ivy at this point. Jiff scored a second goal minutes later and eventually Wardle finished with a hat-trick. His incessant running must have scraped off a few of the stains and dirt on himself. He was unmarked most of the game because of the stench he gave off, and remains to this day, the only player who needs a shower before a game.

WHITE SHORTS WHITE SOCKS

Racism and a last gasp equaliser - 13th September 2003.

A stressed-out weekend if there ever was one. On Friday I was told that on Saturday afternoon, I was due to expect my new midlife crisis fanny magnet which was in the form of a 1979 Lotus Éclat, leather interior - the works. problems occurred as the car was being trailered from Kent. Eventually I was told Tuesday, which pissed me off no end. But amazingly I got a call on the way home from work and was told it was on its way and would be with me at midnight. So, being knackered already, I had to stay up. I got the car took it for a spin and went to sleep at around 2am.

Out big game was a true stress headache, and it was against Mountain Daisy. Our performances had been good, but I was still paranoid and always looking at excuses as to why we won. Pre-match investment was high. I'd just produced some Sassco corner flags by

WHITE SHORTS WHITE SOCKS

using some electrical piping, a Stanley knife and four Sassco prints. And got some water bottles (plain) which made the water taste as if it was from the wear (what do you mean "as if it was").

This game against the Daisy was the biggest test in our forthcoming set of games. And what a test it was. We were getting swamped in the first half and it was not a surprise when they scored. The massive surprise was Jiff equalising within 50 seconds after brilliant work from Staples, who had his best game to date. We went 2-1 up with Wardle grabbing a goal on the break. But they eventually equalised and went 3-2 up. It was at this stage that they Daisy keeper shouted some derogative racial abuse directed towards me. The poor lad has basically fucked his team up now. They will get a heavy fine for it, and he could be banned for a long time. Stupid dickhead. A letter is being sent to the league at this time and should be interesting to see how much balls the league must do anything about it. The referee said she didn't hear it after the game - Bollocks - everyone heard it, and there was a hush on the pitch for a while afterwards. Most of the Daisy lads (don't know them personally) seem okay as most of the teams in the league are. In nearly four years of involvement in local football this is my first real taste of racial abuse.

WHITE SHORTS WHITE SOCKS

Well back to the game - we went 4-2 down which pissed me off big style. This was in the second half and Jif was off injured by now. I stressed the importance of taking your chances in a game, and in this one, we had some embarrassing obvious ones. Yet we dug in deep and after Wardle had missed his usual fair share of good chances, we struck back with Baker opening his account for us. We were on the up. Pressure was constant and we were getting stronger and stronger at the back. In the dying minutes we broke the offside trap and Staples megged the 'keeper (how pleasing is that) for his first goal this season (and probably his last). Good stuff. Both teams had chances, and it was a genuine bruiser of a game. I walked away still thinking about the number of chances we keep missing (Wardle anyone?).

The biggest thing that disappointed me was the general attitude of the Daisy lads after I'd sent the letter in. Most of them see Boothy in the pub and most were saying they can't wait for a rematch after what I'd said about them. It's almost as if I'd done something wrong by making a complaint about racial abuse. Typical attitude really. I did half expect it. But that's the problem overall. my lads on a night out would probably do the same if some Asian or African person called them. That's the way of the world. Just because they know me well, wouldn't mean they'd not give racial abuse. But I know they wouldn't if I was there.

And that's my general attitude towards race. I am not an honorary white, but that doesn't mean I'm insular. When Asians class themselves as Indian and Pakistani, they tend to get religious and shun the white man. I'm the opposite. I'm fully integrated and always will be, but until racism has been completely stamped out in every form, that's the day I'll call myself British and not Indian - unfortunately, that day will never ever happen.

[note added September 2024 - Looking back at this, it's amazing how time changes things, including society. The feeling of being a person just living in a foreign land is long gone, as society has moved on, even having a (albeit crap) Indian PM. I'd pass Norman Tebbit's "cricket test" now.]

I remember when I watched a cup final and was standing next to Anth Mouat who was spurting out racial abuse to one of the white lads on the pitch (I think he was slightly dark skinned). And I still think now why I didn't say anything to Anth Mouat. I just stood there like a muppet not saying anything. Not even a "fuck off you fat bastard" to him.

It did come to a head later. I seem to recall him saying that he wasn't a fan of coloured people or immigrants and then said that he spoke to me and our boy because we were okay. I publicly told him to fuck off and never talk to me again. Made my feelings known quite clearly and I think he was taken a back. Typical though, he started to talk a week or so later and never made a racial comment to this day. I think that's what needs to be done. Any form of racism must be harshly stamped on, so everyone knows it's unacceptable. As for my political views. I am fiercely anti-immigration. My parents came as economic migrants purely. Modern days If an Iraqi needs asylum, he needs to go to Jordan or Pakistan and doesn't need to come to the UK. According to the UN, I think he needs to go to the first friendly nation.

WHITE SHORTS WHITE SOCKS

Mid-life crisis fanny magnet problems - 16th September 2003.

I had a tasking weekend. Heavily stressed. On Sunday I'd practically blown up my precious Éclat. I tried to rewire the radio in to avoid any more singing to myself while in the car. Problem is I shorted a wire, and it burnt through. Smoke everywhere. Worst was yet to come. I started the ignition and oil was spurting everywhere. I'd burnt through the oil pressure pipe, and I couldn't get it back on! I was nearly in tears. Call the RAC and after some persuading, he looked under the bonnet and found where the pipe came from. He told me to plug it up with a screw of the same size. Did it, but now I'm so paranoid the car will conk out. Way to stressed.

On the Tuesday I was driving back from work and all I heard was a loud yell which sounded like a fire engine going past. It was Alfie. He'd spotted the new

WHITE SHORTS WHITE SOCKS

Lotus Éclat I'd just bought. As far as football today, not a lot to report on. Only important thing was the unveiling of the Lotus Éclat. I surged down the back end of the field behind the complex to a standing ovation. I blew the horn, which sounds exactly like it is – a 1970's high pitched squeal. And then the piece de resistance, the vacuum pop-up lights. Fantastic. I didn't do any web updates tonight.

Way too stressed out.

Crashing back to Earth - 20th September 2003.

I had a decent night's sleep. I used a method (as read in the Reader's Digest) which involves clenching all the parts of the body in succession for thirty seconds and then slowly letting go. This was done just before I went to bed, and it worked. My son, Arjan was at his grandmother's, so I didn't really have to rush around in the morning neither. Her indoors was fast asleep, but I got a text message in the morning requesting a cup of coffee (what's wrong with banging your fucking feet on the floor love like you normally do?).

An away day to the Cliff. Last season, our modern-day adventures and performances started with a 2-1 win there. They were called the New Derby then, but this season (like us) chose to change their name. I fired up the yellow Mid Life Crisis Fanny Magnet Lotus Éclat and juggernauted my way to the ground, with the help of an Autoroute Map. Whizzing down the A194, then the A1300 and at the ground – piece of piss. Boothy was already there along with Wardle and Stubba. Greenwell soon turned up playing his diva music – I'm sure he had some Donna Summer in his car and a Cher CD. Also, I celebrated the fact that I found my missing water bottle in the back of Greenwell's car and that Boothy had shitloads of white socks on him. Last night I was panicking as I only had a few and was sure we should have had more than enough.

This time we turned up at the Cliff high on confidence and brilliant morale. So, it wasn't really a surprise when we suffered a deserved walloping. I think most of the boys were way too overconfident. I wasn't entirely sure how the game would go as I am ever the pessimist. Harper also turned up, not to watch, but borrow a CD off me full of porn. He gave his usual moral support by slagging off Muers. But control yourself Mr Harper. It was Muers who picked you out with a pinpoint "bend it like Boothy" cross for you to score your only goal for us. So, you own him one. As far as moral support goes, most of the lads should call The Samaritans after their eventual 5-0 defeat. The 5-0 could have been much worse. Out of 12 players involved, only Watson was outstanding and Greenwell to a lesser extent. I can't believe the amount of one on

WHITE SHORTS WHITE SOCKS

ones, Watty saved. Truly mind blowing which shows that he is one of the unsung heroes. He was missing for quite a few games last season, otherwise we would have finished further up the league (by one place).

But looking at the overall performance, we won't win games if we don't work hard. True we can score goals from anywhere and unexpectedly, but when we're chasing a game it's bloody impossible. Our philosophy at the latter stages of last season was not to come off the pitch without a battle. This time we barely had time to load our ammo. It seemed like the horrible mid-season, last season when the grounds we played on used to be soaking because we'd had the piss taken out of us. Today, players failed to close the opposition and allowed them to take the piss. My simple ideas on football are when closing, a player should be prepared for the fact that the opposition will dink the ball past them and turn on the ball. There's no point in someone like Jiff hurtling half the length of the field to lunge in and make himself look like a moron. When we don't have the ball, the team should close ranks and man-to-man mark, very tightly. In that way we'll win the ball back. Also, there were too many long balls in the wrong direction. Staples was struggling as the service to him was dire. Dixon had a genuine nightmare along with Galey. Both seemed completely out of their depth. The midfield was taking the goal kicks. Wardle sometimes looks like a big soft puff. Mav did okay, Stubba did okay and so did Boothy, but the lack of his left foot meant he got himself into trouble instead of clearing it first time. Muers made a return and didn't do too badly. He had to replace Baker (injured) just before the half time whistle and the second half saw him in midfield. Ironically, he didn't do badly.

We'd lost the game at that time, but at least he got his head to the ball and gave a better option. But as far as testing the goalkeeper, we just didn't even bother. One thing we could rely on in the last few games was our shooting opportunities. This time it let us down. It's back to basics lads. When we lose the ball, we do nothing but to win it back by non-stop pressure, even on the goalkeeper. We must rush the opposition into making mistakes and we must capitalise on them. We did it against Sandhills and we did it against Mountain Daisy. What we must do now – is do it against our local rivals, the Redhouse SCUM.

WHITE SHORTS WHITE SOCKS

New Tango please - 27th September 2003.

The bullshit started midweek. Mav got a boot in the chest when it was the turn of my six-a-side team, known as Dadcheck, after my workplace sponsored it to take on Jon Wardle's Southwell (known as the Farmers). We lost and our 2-1 defeat depressed me quite a bit. Mav also got sent off for swearing at the ref, and Jon Wardle also got in on the act with some passionate complaints to the referee. I wasn't surprised that Mav didn't turn up on Saturday. A text to Jiff said his ribs were bruised. After a depressing defeat against The Cliff, we needed an immediate comeback against the Redhouse Scum. Now the scum weren't half as good as they were in earlier seasons, but they played as a team and had been going through a decent spell in the league. Our lot turned up and got battered again, despite playing with a brand-new Adidas Tango ball (yep, bought for 50 euros from Deutschland). If the Redhouse lot were a bit more accomplished, then the score line would have been far greater than our walloping off the Cliff. I took last week's defeat and blanks fired by Wardle and Jiff as a one off.

It's clear that it wasn't though. Both fired blanks. I gave the fat twat a warning before the game that I needed some of his anger he uses midweek, but to no avail. He was useless. Normally he'll score from anywhere but this time he was impotent. Jiff was the same. He failed to use his pace and missed an obvious chance to equalise (straight at the keeper).

We had a bright start. Most of the side-line said we'd walk it. But I was never so sure. The minute Redhouse scored, it was all over. Defensively we were inept.

Couldn't clear a ball to save our lives. Midfield was non-existent. No one won a ball. Baker was quiet, Greenwell was quiet and Boothy was quite shite. Playing in his usual centre half role, he seemed out of sorts. Pearson was available as he'd changed his job (or got sacked) but I'm not sure what he thought he'd turned up for. Watson proved how good a keeper he was by saving plenty of shots and being decisive. But it's not enough that we turn up for each game saying that Watty played well. There were major suggestions about team changes etc. But to cut the bullshit, it's all about hard work. Why are we allowing other teams to string four or five passes together when they don't allow us to? Hard work, that's why.

It's very depressing. I've never felt like this before, but the reason is that we know we can do it and we've proven it. But like I said to William Harper months and months ago – we do it with this team. No major additions, no major changes because when the shit hits the fan (like it did last season), the likes of Dixon, Muers, Greenwell and co. will be there. It's just a case of how much pride they have now.

Ball looked good though. . .

WHITE SHORTS WHITE SOCKS

Faith restored - 11th October 2003.

Faith was restored. Over the last few weeks, it's been known that a lot of decent lads were interested in signing for us, but I held off in any more signings. The situation is that the current bunch of lads are all regulars, are all reliable and all (apart from Stubba) pay their subs regularly. These new lads would probably be the same - but I've always said, "we'll win something or be successful with these or not win with these - but the team stays the same." I've been criticised a bit from different quarters saying we need more subs for competition for places. But the fact remains, it's amateur footy and all the lads have just about cemented their places and pay good money to keep it going. And it's not as if the substitutes we have are just muppets who get put on just because they are there. The substitutes are just as competent on the lads on the pitch, if not a little inconsistent.

WHITE SHORTS WHITE SOCKS

Now, Silksworth Catholic Club are exemplary, but they lost some of their key players after a good season last season. A season where they walloped up 6-2 at home and shockingly 7-0 away. The away game saw me, my brother, Tarnjit (aka Fatboy), Anth Mouat the goat and the Tash playing - so 7-0 was probably a good result.

The usual pre-match build up. No pegs. According to Wayne, Boothy rang him to tell him that Fatboy was going to bring them, but Fatboy heard that Wayne was going to bring them, so he didn't...blah blah blah. Dixon was late on the pitch, Pearson, who was called up and told me he'd be there, did not show making him possibly the most unreliable player in Sunderland. I still don't know why he wasn't there, could be a genuine reason, but don't know until I get a call or text. Greenwell and co. looked spaced out. Jiff, who I didn't expect to be there as he had a cup game away in the afternoon, turned up. Stubba was late which was scary considering that Watty was absent having just come off the aeroplane at 8am in the morning (so why weren't you there? No excuse Watty). Stubba did eventually turn up and we all calmed down as they expected me to go in goal - the goat would have been better.

So, with all this mass disorganisation, it's probably

not surprising we won. I had a good team out there. We went 1-0 down with their first attack and I expected another demoralising defeat. But then the turning point. The Catholic's decided that my new 50-euro Adidas Tango ball, despite being FIFA Approved, wasn't good enough. So, they replaced it with a Mitre Shit Kicker. Almost at once we scored an equaliser through Jiff. Eventually we went 2-1 up with a fortuitous goal from Jiff again. I was livid that he decided to pass when he was through on goal. But a bit of luck saw him and Staples pressure in a goal. But it would have been a simple strike, but for some reason Jiff decided to pass when in on goal. They equalised from an easy header from a corner. Baker was marking a 6-footer and until we use a little bit of common sense, we're going to struggle.

Second half saw us take the lead with another Jiffy strike. It was Wardle who put us 4-2 up before Silks pulled one back. Again, through Wardle, who was having his best game for a while, we struck again, and Wardle was overall unlucky to not grab a hat-trick or more. He had some excellent shots, three of which just squirmed wide. Silks scored their final goal after three of our defenders missed the ball, but the scoring ended, and we'd just secured our first win in four games.

WHITE SHORTS WHITE SOCKS

All the players played well. Dixon was on the bench and Muers was on the wing in the first half. I replaced Muers with Dixon in the second half to a little bit of criticism, but at the end of the day, there are certain people who have cemented their places and Muers isn't one of them. If I held that view, then Dixon wouldn't be shifted after his Hollymere performance, a game where Muers had a nightmare. But then Dixon really hasn't recovered after his "shit on the shoe" incident away to Ivy. Gourlay was back in his first game since the 4-0 away win against Ivy and was truly outstanding. Not a single pass was wasted, and he was directly involved in more than one goal. Mav at centre half was strong and aggressive and was the perfect foil for Booth who had a good outing. Stubba was a little shaky in goal, but overall was highly competent and agile, but then having pure 99% Orangutan DNA makes it just a swing in the jungle for the boy. Galey had a good game, but the midfield struggled just a little bit. Being unable to cope with the long high ball is one thing but being unable to win the second ball -the knock down, was unacceptable. Baker and Greenwell had average games. Both were contrasting, Greenwell's excellent when we haven't got the ball and Baker's good when we do have it, so it's a good partnership overall. Staples had a classic game while Muers didn't do too bad. Dixon was similar

WHITE SHORTS WHITE SOCKS

when he came on. Up front though, Jiff and Wardle were outstanding. Jiff got his hat-trick while Wardle should have got his. Wardle's passing was sometimes a bit astray. Most of his passes hit the opposition players directly and I did make the comment that most of the opposition weren't as fat as him, so he could somehow widen his pass angle a bit.

A good game. My faith is restored. We went on a bad run last season and never recovered, but the players we had last season were lacking. This season, the three new lads, Maven, Baker and Dickinson have plugged the obvious gaps in Defence, Midfield and Attack. I still don't think we have it in us to go away to the likes of the Club and get something because it's a proper battle out there, but then again, our performances against Sandhills and Mountain Daisy were genuinely outstanding.

Faith renewed - 18th October 2003.

What was the biggest fear before the game? That Watty was missing and Stubba had to go in goal? Muers was going to play the full 90 minutes? Nope…. The fear was that I was the only available substitute.

A fear perfectly illustrated when Staples suffered a bone crunching challenge late in the first. Before I had the chance to get my trackies off and my boots on, he got back to his feet urged on by 10 of his teammates.

But thankfully I wasn't really needed. We simply had an outstanding 90 minutes against SW Gardens. The second half was nothing short of awesome, and with seven goals to add to the opening half's three goals, I didn't really have any complaints.

But the night before, the squad wasn't entirely up to scratch. Both Dixon and Watson were absent. I was well aware of this a long while back, so I knew the team was down to its bare bones. But Galey was also suffering from a cold and would only last one half. So, it was back to the mobile phone list to see who was available. I called the "Tash," the first name on all my lists, but he was out. Keith Mouat, being second, was working, but then I realised that his equally big brother, Paul Mouat, didn't have a game in the afternoon and was quite happy to play.

And for once we didn't really have an incident packed day. Corner flags were up, nets were up as we had some new pegs. This meant we didn't have to trawl around the burnt-out car parts in the corners of the pitch to use objects as pegs.

Muers opened the scoring after some head tennis, but then a period of dominating but nonchalant football saw a little bit of panic. Stubba pulled off a cracking save when we were 1-0 up, but eventually Paul Mouat scored his header followed by Wayne scoring from close range.

The second saw us start the way we ended the first. Greenwell scored again along with a cracking strike from Jiff. Greenwell eventually found his hat-trick and so did Mouaty. Maven also grabbed his first after he was granted so much space. Finally, Wardle did manage to score after he picked up the scraps left by his team, and

WHITE SHORTS WHITE SOCKS

Dave Gourlay should have got on the scoresheet – as should have Boothy. We did well, I really enjoyed it. I was delighted that Mouaty played - and play he did. Three headed goals – all from corners from Muers and Gourlay were perfect. We haven't scored from corners for nearly six months – but to have three in one game was outstanding. Mouaty got his man-of-the-match award, and the team was solid. We had him signed on last season but the team we had was diabolical and I never called upon him as he'd soon get demoralised. The one game he did play in was a 5-1 defeat against Sandhills – and in that one, he threw his weight and height around and was the one outstanding player on the pitch for us.

Faith comes crashing down - 25th October 2003.

8:00am Alarm woke me up and it took me 5 minutes to realise what for? Sassco 11-a-side day of course.

8:05am Watched BBC News. Nothing happening – usual death, chaos, destruction and rain. 8:30am Breakfast. Tea and two slices of plain toast – no butter, etc.

8:45am Got bits ready. Tried to contact Wayne who wasn't answering.

9:00am Fired up the now newly sprayed white Mid Life Crisis Fanny Magnet Aka Le Clit Magnet.

Filled it with petrol and proceeded to travel to Boothy's birds house to pick him up.

9:20am Dangerous route through Ford Estate and Pennywell to pick up Wardle and Stubba. If I was around half an hour later, the Magnet would have been stripped bare (wheels and all), and no doubt Boothy would have been gang raped.

10:00am Arrived on the pitch. Bloody freezing began to get a headache and the usual "why do I really bother" thoughts (also echoed by the rest of the team. Mav, Staples and Watty arrive. Mav wishes the game was called off.

10:10am Dixon and Galey arrive. Dixon's the only one who really doesn't feel the cold.

10:30am Muers Greenwell and Baker are late as always. Sandhills turn up with a vast squad. We're still down to 8 men. Referee looks dodgy. One of those type of guys who probably couldn't get in the Police or Fire service and now is a referee ready to lay down the law.

10:35am We don't need to put our head to the floor to hear the Greenwell mobile turn up. 10:40am Kick off at last

10:43am Goal down in the first minute 10:55am Mav tells ref to fuck off – gets sent off

10:56am Wardle sticks his oar in and says something similar – gets sent off

10:57am Muers gets sent off because he's thick as pig shit. Shame he got sent off early. The referee didn't give me enough time to sub him.

WHITE SHORTS WHITE SOCKS

10:58am Spent the first half defending in some style.
11:10am Soon conceded another one.

11:15am Wayne bollocks Wardle for getting sent off
11:17am Concede more goals

11:18am Wayne bollocks Wardle for getting sent off
11:20am Half time, we're around 3 or 4-0 down.

11:21am Wayne says to me in seriousness, "ere, we can win this…". Staples nearly vomits. 11:22am Boothy wants to jack it in

11:25am Second half starts

11:27am Wayne bollocks Wardle for getting sent off

11:45am Wardle asks the ref to blow his whistle -

Muers ask the referee to "blow on this," pointing to his crotch.

11:50am I'm beginning to hop around, dying for a piss without getting arrested. There's no bush or mound in which I can let one out.

11:55am Don't feel like a piss anymore as the

Sandhills basically took it all out of us.

12:00pm Staples nearly scores when were around 9 or

10 down. Dixon sets him up, but he beats the 'keeper and hits the post.

WHITE SHORTS WHITE SOCKS

12:10pm Watson nominated as man-of-the-match after some mind-bending saves after the full-time whistle blows.

WHITE SHORTS WHITE SOCKS

6-1, cold feet and a runny nose - 1st November 2003.

It's always the same. Last week was diabolical and this week needed to fare better. But at the end of game, all I was left with was cold feet, a runny nose and testicles the size of half-eaten peanuts. Boothy was away, so I had to go cap in hand to the opposition with the team sheet. It wasn't a good read. 6-1 was the final score and it was fully deserved.

The beginnings, as always, was the problem. Again, Wayne turned up late at 10:30pm precisely. This is simply not good. No time for a few wisecracks and a team talk – so no progress in the game. Some other team had already put their nets up, but had to play on a different team, so we didn't even have to put them up. Also, the Echo guy turned up to take a team photo – which was nice, but we struggled to arrange a line up. In the game itself, Jiff missed a cracking chance in the first few minutes, and it was over. We conceded some laughable goals, which could have been prevented. But all in all, the Club were more up for it. We had no time on the ball, and we gave them too much time on the ball. There were no rough tackles, and it wasn't really a dirty game. But with the Club 4-0 up at the interval, they didn't need to.

Half time saw Wayne giving a team talk because to be honest, I really couldn't be arsed. If people aren't going to turn up on time, there's no point in the likes of me, Watty, Boothy, etc. doing all the donkey work. And to top it off, we couldn't even decide on a new captain.

Wardle's recent disgraceful performances meant that he no longer had the respect in terms of footballing. My nomination was, and still is, Watty. But it didn't really matter. No one listens to no one, and they all criticise and whinge at each other. Jiff and Wardle were terrible up front. Midfield didn't fare much better, and the defence was nervous at a push. The final score was going to be 60, but surprisingly, Staples scored his second goal this season. We were up for it now and had opportunities including a clanger from Wardle. But then it's a waste of time going 6-0 down and then learning to be up for it.

Premonitions and a drop out - 8th November 2003.

Well, it's safe to say that the past week has been nothing short of a total nightmare. On Tuesday, we had a cancellation nightmare for the Sassco League and on Thursday, the magnet broke down. But luckily it was only a minor electrical problem which was solved.

So, going into Friday night, I developed my usual temperature before our league encounter away to Low Fell. Ironically last season was the same. I was ill, we had a bit part team with none of our major regulars. Boothy, Mav, Galey and Jiff were all missing. So, Ed Cook and Harper were drafted in….

Waking up on the Saturday morning at 8:00am. I looked directly at my mobile phone and new something was going to happen – and it did. Ed Cook was unable to make it. Mass panic set in. I was going to have to play. But Kelsey came to the rescue with his short notice return to the fold this season. But then the Tash dropped us in it. "I'll be there, I'll be there. Might only play 45 minutes but I'll be there."

No show.

Staples, Kelsey and Watty were the first in. Staples had successfully navigated a three in the bed romp the night before, so he looked a bit rough. Wardle has been trying to pop his bird for nearly three weeks. Rule Number 1 Fatty – if you haven't bust a bird in 72 hours, knock it on the head and move on (no wonder he's been playing shite).

The team we had wasn't too bad and was clearly good enough. Fatty was in defence with Stubba. I was right back and Gourlay left back. Kelsey was right wing and up front we had Muers and Dixon. Today was the day to deliver, and they didn't.

We equalised near the end of the first half with a mazy run from Dixon resulting in Kelsey scoring with his left foot. It was all for the taking. We'd been dominating and they'd scored with their first attack. But we simply couldn't convert dominance into goals. Dixon and Muers simply failed as attackers and based on this performance will always be undecided players.

They went ahead just before half time when we

called offside. I was playing the lad on (I think) so I'll take the flak – but isn't it common sense to have a look to see where I am before screaming "Offffsssssssssiiiiiiiide referee." This time there was no Harper to shout out.

Second half was crap. They went ahead with their first chance of the second and eventually ended up beating us 4-1. Deserved I'd say – they were clinical, and we weren't.

We had a bonding session in the pub down the road from the ground afterwards. But the landlord said to Kelsey, "We want nee drugs or funny business in here mate…" Obviously knows him.

Went home, went to sleep. My legs were aching.

WHITE SHORTS WHITE SOCKS

Lack of interest - 15th November 2003.

It seems to be getting worse every week. It's almost as if no one seems interested anymore. We had a major player crisis. I spent almost all day on Friday searching for available players. Eventually I got two, but late on Friday night, both were unavailable. Then Gourlay rings up and decides he's not fit after all after waiting all week. Complete disaster. Most players on the team seem not to realise what a complete ball ache me, Watty and Boothy must go through. Also, the incompetent league is going bankrupt. Now how the fuck can it go bankrupt. What is the league actually paying? We pay affiliation fees, we pay pitch fees, we pay the referee. If they turn around and say it's on trophies – they need to be shot. How can a non-profit league justify purchasing trophies when no real money is coming in. Completely diabolical. I run my own leagues and cost everything up so to make sure that enough is available for trophies.

WHITE SHORTS WHITE SOCKS

Anyway, back to the game. We just managed to get 11 players when Muers was available. We were lucky he was, because he got butt-fucked by a bird with a strap on dildo the night before. He literally got kidney bashed and could barely walk. But it's probably not the first time its happened so he was used to it. Maven had broken his leg in two places the week before so unfortunately, he's ruled out for the near future. Jiff's injured and Wayne was missing due to his grandmother's funeral.

As for the game itself. We dominated the opening and missed four clear cut chances. Kelsey's mate was up front, playing as a ringer and decided to miss three of them. Dixon also missed one in the first half – but he nearly scored from a stunning free-kick only to see the keeper palm it onto the post. We did break the deadlock when staples scored from a stunning strike. But they equalised at the end of the first half when Jon Wardle, waddling around like a fat twat, was supposed to be plugging the gaps in midfield.

I couldn't say much at half time. Told the lads we'd lost it in the first. We simply can't allow chances to go begging like that. True enough in the second, with the wind behind them, Shiney went ahead. Surprisingly we equalised from Dixon and just when we were taking control of the game, Muers took a limp wrested, shirt lifter corner which resulted in them hurtling down the field and Kelsey giving away a penalty. He was subsequently sent off for threatening the referee. They scored and eventually finished the game 4-2 winners.

The afters for the game were disastrous. One net was taken down and the other wasn't. I told the lads if it isn't down then we're jacking it in. Needless to say, it wasn't despite me threatening Stubba to take the fucker down or to fuck off. What pissed me off more was Boothy taking Wardle and Stubba to the pitch to take the net down and both saying no. I would have told the bastards to fuck off and walk home.

I was genuinely pissed off and really can't be arsed anymore.

Guilt of racism - 18th November 2003.

It was D-DAY for the resolving of the racial issues in our game against Mountain Daisy. The opposition team had completely denied any occurrence of the "Fuck off you paki bastard!" comment. Including the referee. So, it was down to me Boothy and Watty to go to Durham FA for 6pm to resolve it. We were early and eventually the Daisy arrived with everyone including the referee – how fucking obvious is that the referee, Joanne, was clearly a "homer."

The committee asked us questions and we were frighteningly honest. The crux of the argument was that why would I make such a complaint. We had clawed it back to 4-4 against a team which had walloped us 15-1 last season and were on a high. Also, with nearly four to five years of non-stop involvement with football, this was the first time a complaint was made.

I even mentioned that we had loads of witnesses

including "a lad from the complex." which was Simon. One of the committee guys perked his head up and said that this Si could be a valid independent witness – almost giving me ammunition to fire against the Daisy. But no. I said Si plays in my leagues and my Thursday team so he wouldn't be independent. "It's our word against their word – simple as that."

We were all removed from the committee room while they decided. The Daisy lads seemed okay as we were having minor chit chat. It's a shame really because I'd be responsible for any of my teams' actions if they did something similar and to be honest wouldn't deny it. An example is Wardle's sending offs. It his own fault, the fat cunt.

The committee dragged us in and announced that Daisy was guilty, and all the paperwork would be sent out. And that's it.

Later on, during the six-a-side, we had a hastily arranged team meeting. The Sassco 11-a-side seem to be rapidly disintegrating. Regulars such as Mav and Jiff are injured which meant draft players coming in. Also, the failure of anyone taking responsibility for the nets was diabolical. We agreed to get a new net in time for our next home game – we'll see if it happens.

WHITE SHORTS WHITE SOCKS

WHITE SHORTS WHITE SOCKS

Point blank in the face for Kelsey - 22nd November 2003.

We had two new faces for Saturday's game against Britannia. Jason Amour, who had done outstandingly well for his team in the six-a-side league and used to have a metal bolt in is dick. And also, a welcome return for Jeff Clark, who had played quite a few games last season.

He didn't play much this season due to driving lessons. Jeff also has perfected the art of running without moving his arms. I had to play as well and changed the team around so that Kelsey partnered Dixon up front.

The game mirrored the last game with dominance in the first half. Countless opportunities were missed, and they scored in the last minute of the half to go 1-0 ahead. Second half saw us wilting a bit. While we were listening to England winning in the RWC, we were suffering the usual arguments. I let loose midway in the second half and had a slanging match with stand in captain, Wayne. Bloody ironic. He said bott all during the game and only responded to some verbals. Dixon had what you could call, nothing short of a mare. The lad's had so many opportunities to cement his position up front but simply hasn't taken it. The one funny aspect of the game was Kelsey getting walloped point blank in the face by the ball. He stood up and I thought he was going to chin the lad who did it (who was clearly frightened). The referee called him over and I thought Kels was going to get a yellow card. If he did, he probably wouldn't have remembered his own name! Never mind. We eventually lost 3-0 and now seem to have come to terms with the fact that we are quite below par. But saying that, we had Mav, Jiff and Wardle in the team, which was defeated 61 by the Club, so no excuses there neither.

Mud caked, but victorious - 29th November 2003.

It was really pissing it down. Probably the start of the miserable season. Caked in mud we came off the pitch reasonably content with a good, if not kamikaze, performance.

We were playing at Ryhope, so it was the usual pre-match conference in McDonalds. I got my usual sausage and pancakes along with tea and a hash brown. We had a bit of a change in the team. Up front it was new lad, Gareth Brazier partnered by Dave Gourlay. Gash, as he's more commonly known, was introduced originally as a referee from the six-a-side leagues. I was aware he wanted to play for us and asked a few lads of their opinion of him. It was positive so I invited him in. A good choice. He's up for it and very reliable. The rest of the team was reasonably the same. Stubba had made a return after I threatened him with Durham FA. To everyone's shock, he produced his kit and a tenner on Thursday, making him available for Saturday. We originally thought he wasn't going to be there, but never mind. Greenwell also turned up late.

Pitch side there was no referee, so Muers and Wardle (both banned) spent time talking to a larger young woman, a person who collects Sassco footballers. Rumours are going around that Stubba, had secured it into the young lady. Stubba denies the rumours, but he had a glint in his eye and was in a cheerful mood.

Anyway, with the rain hurtling down, we raced into a two-goal lead. Gourlay and Gash, the GGs up front were outstanding. True we were playing against a weak team, but then again, we dominated in our last two games but failed to deliver. Studio grabbed one back after some laughable defending. But it was only a blip. The eventual score saw Gash grabbing two, Greenwell scoring, Galey – out of position, scoring and Gourlay grabbing a hattrick. I came on myself for Staples in the first, moments after Stubba had to replace a tender Watson in goal. During the game itself, we genuinely should have scored more, but it seemed as if we were trying to walk it into the net. Gash had an outstanding game. His normal position is central midfield, but he transferred to striker with no real problem. He stayed onside with no problems, something we've struggled with, and passed the ball and won it exceptionally well. For the first half, the referee was one of their guys and for the second, it was Fatty. And he was diabolical.

Good result but, most of all, enjoyable. If we were playing away to the Club and it was pissing it down, and we'd got slaughtered, I'd have a different view – but who cares.

WHITE SHORTS WHITE SOCKS

Running like clockwork - 6th December 2003.

For the first time in ages, everything ran like clockwork. All players were on time for a change. I got a tenner from Greenwell, which he owed. The team had one extra player, so I didn't need to get my kit on. The nets were put up perfectly – even Baker helped put the pegs in (amazing!). And we had a reasonably good performance. Reasonably good because we identified the two goals we conceded after being two goals ahead.

We went 1-0 ahead with a Wayne Greenwell free kick, which Gash cleverly jumped over as it was going straight in the net. We were 1-0 up and quite comfortable. The half time saw Dixon coming on for Jeff Clark, but there weren't any other major changes. The team was balanced with Stubba, Boothy, Kelsey and Galey in defence. Stapes, Digga on the flanks. Greenwell and Baker in the middle with Gash and the returning Jiff up front. Jiff showed his early promise but probably needs another game to be really into it. Muers was there as well and got some of his mud pies on target while standing on the side lines – same can't be said about his shooting. The bald bastard is the only one who hasn't contributed towards his fine and will be banned until he does. Fatty turned up looking like Piltdown man and paid a tenner towards his £33, so things are looking up. Even Stubba paid £1 in his subs.

We went 2-0 up in the second half. Jiff missed, but Gash was on hand to finish off. But then Hollymere scored. Boothy needlessly gave away a corner and they took advantage. They scored again and this was soon after Gash could have put us 3-1 up. It was going to be one of those days. Gash and Jiff missed several gilt-edge chances before a long clearance from Boothy was latched onto and despatched by Gash with around ten minutes left. There were no other goals to talk about as we'd secured our second consecutive win. The nets came down quickly. ALL the team mucked in which was superb.

Team spirit really can't get any better. The crack in the changing rooms was okay as everyone hung around for a while. We also heard that Muers had been body slammed by a fat bird with a strap on dildo - the the

WHITE SHORTS WHITE SOCKS

world is your oyster.

WHITE SHORTS WHITE SOCKS

Eleven goals down - 13th December 2003.

RnB music. What's it all about. Now I personally think it's completely shite and people only buy it and listen to it because they think it's cool.

What a week, eh? On Wednesday I got arrested for having a fight with the wife. Got locked up in a cell from 8:30 in the morning until 1:00pm in the afternoon. Got cautioned, mug shot taken, DNA taken. Moved out of the house, went to me mothers. Got 32 text messages off the wife, ignored most of them. Eventually she begged me back. Thursday night. Magnet battery failed. Tried to charge it with these shitty jump leads from B&Q which wouldn't work properly. So, after 45 minutes of trying. I cut the bastards and taped em on. Laughing. Car started – but then the bastard exhaust dropped off. RAC guy fixed it. Friday, while getting a new battery for it, the bastard exhaust dropped again. But this time the local garage guy fixed it properly.

WHITE SHORTS WHITE SOCKS

So footy on Saturday was a drop in the ocean. We had the bare 11 players. Only problem was that half were spaced out. Watty was done in from his works night out. But with Jase missing, we only had one centre half if Stubba was to go in. Stubba himself requested a berth on the subs bench. Now, any cynical twat would think that he hadn't brought his subs. But he did and was genuinely under the weather. Baker was truly spaced out and he brought with him his two mates who were also spaced out and drinking on the side lines.

Game started and we made four errors in the first fifteen minutes. So, in the traditional Sassco way, we were 4-0 down. Watty nearly attacked Gourlay for some reason, then Watty started to wave his arm round requesting to be subbed. Well on the side lines it was only Fatty Wardle and Baker's two mates – one of whom was completely doing me heed in by wanting to come on. Turns out that he isn't supposed to be bad player at all – but he was well pissed.

Second half saw it get worse. We had minor chances but even then, it simply didn't work. We were 11- 0 down by the time of the final whistle. The infamous Joanne was refereeing us, but ironically didn't book any one of us for a change (but then again, we weren't playing against the Mountain Daisy).

WHITE SHORTS WHITE SOCKS

You gorra laugh though. I don't mind people getting pissed out of their skulls on Friday nights, and who am I to tell anyone how to go about their own social life, but when due to play on a Saturday morning, I'll eventually drop the players who are always pissed because we clearly can't have performances like that again. T'was diabolical.

WHITE SHORTS WHITE SOCKS

Gourlay quits - 20th December 2003.

Me and Boothy had ironed out some rules which were to take effect in the New Year. Draconian? yes, of course, but that's the way it must be.

I expected it to be a calamitous organisational nightmare. Staples and Kelsey were due to be missing but both had kit. Jeff had his kit from ages ago, and little known to us, Baker went AWOL as well. Well anyway, Staples turned up, we had to send Watty to get Kelsey's unwashed strip and Boothy brought Stubba's top. Stubba was on crutches on Thursday, but amazingly declared himself fit. Well to you and me, the last thing I'd declare Stubba would be as "fit", because he is by far the ugliest person in the squad (if not the League).

Luckily, we had a decent squad together with me and Stubba on the bench and a return of the Fatty. We bunged him in at right back to keep himself out of trouble in a game which was eventful to say the least on a muddy but playable pitch, with a Geordie referee who no one really understood.

Ivy house. We'd beaten them heavily on our last meeting, but after our 11-0 walloping, there's no way we'd class ourselves as decent. For the team line up itself, Jase made a welcome return as well after two games absent. Also, with the last result and some absentees, the team was changed a bit. Gourlay and Digga were placed up front. Now poor Digga's been roundly criticised by all including me the most for not putting it away as a striker. Against Ivy, I thought, why not put him alongside Gourlay – a player he combines well with and pop him in attack against a weak team. It failed unfortunately.

Both lads didn't do well enough and true, you can criticise the service, but in some games, you need to make a difference yourselves. Too many times we slowed down quick breaks by Gourlay turning on himself and too many times he passed the ball in front of the opposition's goal area when he knows fine well that he's got an accurate shot on himself. I farmed Gash out to the right wing where to be honest he didn't make a huge difference. Ironically, I was dirtier than him and I was standing on the side-lines. Talking of dirty. The main talking point was the tackle incident against Boothy. Not so much the tackle, but the fact that he fell flat on his face which was lathered in mud. Same happened to Greenwell.

In the game itself, they opened the scoring in the second half. There was one of their guys who was dancing around all our tackles, and it resulted in two more goals. Disaster. When 1-0 down, I told Digga to move to right back and switch with Fatty. I got one hell of a look from Digga, but the fact is in the last 13 games (inc. this one) he's only scored one goal. The run of good form before that saw him scoring three v Hollymere and one v Sandhills back in August and the start of September. So, attack is definitely not his position.

With Fatty up front, it didn't really change much as they'd scored two goals. But suddenly it became different. The minute they scored the third, we got down and dirty and started to play to our strengths. Fatty running through scored two goals to make it 3-2. It looked promising with five minutes left. But unfortunately, Jason gave away a penalty and they ended the tie with a 4-2 away win. Unfortunate, but that's the way it goes. Staples needs to receive a mention this time. Despite playing with the shirt now, with the aid of mud, twice his size, he played like a true captain. Battling for every lost cause and putting so much effort into it – nice one little fella.

All we've got to hope for this next year is that we fire on all cylinders like we did at the start of the season. Thankfully Wardle is back, but disappointingly, his replacements simply haven't delivered and that is a worry. If Wardle won't score, Sassco won't score. Sad footnote was Dave Gourlay deciding to quit the team due to the infighting and problems. Shame, we've lost a good player there.

New Year walloping - 10th January 2004.

Well, the first welcome of the new year was a walloping off the Cliff. I'm slowly getting increasingly demoralised about the whole situation. We seem to be struggling with players constantly and are essentially lambs to the slaughter. We did manage to get a team out, which also included me. Now normally I don't really want to play, but I was glad I did. Beats loitering on the side-lines getting depressed. The team was still missing Muers, Kelsey, Jiff and Mav, but at least Wardle was playing as a legit player. But to be honest, he was totally shite.

Pre match organisation was getting worse. Baker turned up without any shorts, Greenwell turned up without a kit....

So, the eventually lashing - can't remember if it was 6-0 or 7-0 was fully expected. We were far too deep in defence. Me Boothy, Jase and Galey. But complaints from the attack fell on deaf ears. They did fuck all up front. They didn't even have a shot on goal. Cliff were highly organised, physical and more importantly, up for it. Baker, Galey and Greenwell's attitude is slowly getting to me. Galey and Greenwell do sort of have an excuse that they're busy picking other people up, but Baker's attitude is nothing short of poor. He simply isn't a Sassco warrior and doesn't understand the deep lying loyalties of the team. Yeah, were shit, yeah, we couldn't organise a piss up, etc. But the team comes from the six-a-side leagues and has developed into a solid unit. I said at the back end of the season, we win it with this lot or don't win anything at all. That philosophy stays the same and the core of the team are there and always have been there.

Mountain Daisy defeat - 17th January 2004

The report is by Michael Booth

Throughout the week, it was pissing down which left our fixture with the Mountain Daisy in doubt. Several players were unavailable due to various reasons working, injured. So thought Saturday was going to be a shambles. Sangha rang me and said he could not make it either on Saturday (looking after the young one), so I ventured to Washington on Friday evening to collect the kits. Rang around / texted a few players on late Friday evening to make sure they would be there and to meet at 10pm at

MacDonald's, Ryhope. Davinder told me that Billy Harper (Tash) would be turning up, not believing him I phoned Harper myself and he confirmed that he would be there on Saturday at the designated meeting point. Finally sorted.

Woke up on Saturday morning to find the weather

terrible as normal, slight drizzle and cold. Set off and picked Wardle / Stubba up from the heart of Pennywell, sounding my horn at his door, too scared to get out of my house in case I got lynched. Stubba still dressed in his clubbing gear with his flares badge pinned to his trousers appeared from Wardle's with Wardle clutching his back as he walked to the car. Told Stubba he would be in goal today as Watson had broken his finger and Dov was not there either. Whinged "Am I f**k going in goal, you daft c**t, Wardle then suggested that he was too injured to play out and that he would take the goalkeepers jersey. Our top goal scorer in goal scary thought......

Met others at MacDonald's around 10pm, Was amazed when Muers turned up with a crisp £10 note for his pitch fees, inspected the note looked real. Told others that we were waiting for Harper to show, there exact words were "He won't turn up", and sure enough it was 10:10am and still no sign. We headed off to the ground (Ryhope Rec the place where we had earlier in the season beat Ivy House and Studio 2000) without him. We were greeted by the Daisy lads who informed us that the referee had inspected the pitch and that our game would go ahead unlike the Ivy House v The Club match which was due to be played on the next pitch to us. We had the bare bones so selecting the team was not

WHITE SHORTS WHITE SOCKS

particular hard, but the positions were difficult as people were moaning especially about Wardle in goal. But what else could we do. Stubba was told to play centre half injured or not injured as no-one else would take the responsibility. Muers returned to the fold after his lengthy ban, or has he been too busy shagging fat sally. However, he started on the right wing.

Noticed that the referee was a certain Barry Gordon, the guy who totally ruined our game v The Sandhill by sending Muers, Wardle and Mav off for dissent. I warned our players to keep their mouths shut and watch their language.... would they listen? The Daisy line was packed with subs, and a huge gathering of players from The Club, whilst our line consisted of only Keith Brazier.

The game was balanced at 0-0 for about 20 minutes with neither side really creating much. An individual error by Baker gifted the Daisy the lead, Baker blamed Wardle for not coming off his line quick enough, but he aint a keeper and he is playing in goal cos we are short so no blame should be pinned on him. Anyway, it was soon 2-0, as heads seemed to drop after the first goal had been conceded. Muers covering back for Stubba, who was on and off the pitch injured wiped a Daisy player out in the penalty area Penalty 3-0.

WHITE SHORTS WHITE SOCKS

Half-time, Muers requested to play up-front, but I told him to continue to stay on the right. Stubba did not make the 2nd half too injured to carry on. The pitch was now starting to get worse as the game went on. Baker disagreed with a decision given by the referee, and despite been told to shut up by his team-mates continued to demonstrate with dissent, before the referee could produce a card, he stormed off the pitch. The referee finally showed a red card. To the disappointment of the rest of the team and the Daisy lads who all shook their heads that the way Baker carried on. Down to 9 men now and 3-0 down. Sassco created a few opportunities with Muers doing well down the right and making pin-point crosses but no-one on the end of them. The Daisy broke in numbers and used their extra men effectively and scored 4 more goals to condemn Sassco to another defeat. Gash also was booked for dissent towards the referee.

Anyway, not many league games left now and let's hope we beat the Geordies in the final!!

Footnote by Davinder Sangha. You know something? at a push I could have made it. I had to drop our lass off at the airport at 9am and had the young un in tow. I could have taken him to my mothers for a few hours, but I simply couldn't be arsed. Why?

WHITE SHORTS WHITE SOCKS

you ask. I'll tell you why. It's pissing down, half the team won't turn up with their kit or subs. We're playing away to Mountain Daisy; the pitch is waterlogged and we're gonna get fucked. Four or five months ago, come rain or nuclear fucking holocaust, I'd be there. Simply aint up for it anymore. It's also ridiculous that discipline broke down. Gash said he didn't want to play in a position, Stubba didn't want to play centre half etc. It's all bollocks man.

WHITE SHORTS WHITE SOCKS

Team meeting - 20th January 2004.

After Saturday's debacle, I decided to call a compulsory team meeting at the complex on Tuesday. I told Dixon, Watson, Staples and Boothy that they didn't really have to be there because their attitude was second to none. Everyone turned up, apart from Baker and Galey. Baker is now out of the squad. He owes too much money; his attitude is diabolical and it's bringing me down trying to get him to conform. Shame really, he is by far one of our most outstanding players this season and will be a loss. But on reflection, if I wanted someone there who didn't pay their subs, etc. I'd ask Corby to come in.

The meeting was plain and blunt. All were there: Staples, Watty, Stubba, Kelsey, Muers, Greenwell, Gash, Jase, Robason, Jeff Clark and Fatty. I told em all what they owed and amazingly, they all didn't flinch or disagree. It's like last season when the team was gonna fold and I told em the only option was if all chipped in. We also talked about attitude and turning up on time. Greenwell and Stubba were cited for that. I also spoke to Galey on the phone before the meeting and made it clear that I expected him on time and not to fuck off after each game without paying the subs. It was a good meeting and

I'm reasonably confident for the final, now. Robason is going to be there so that's a huge boost as we lack a commanding centre half since Mav got injured.

A bright day, a brilliant performance - 7th February 2004

It was a good day for football. Cold, yes, but bright and reminiscent of the summer days to come ahead. We also had our Ken Atkinson final to look forward to in the midweek. But as far as squad system was going, I expected a small turn out. Two regulars, Stapes and Jase were missing, Baker had been hounded out due to unpaid fines, and as always, I didn't really expect the Tash to turn up. I had asked him, like I asked twice before, but on them occasions, he simply didn't turn up.

But lo and behold, he did, along with Kelsey and John Hunt. The Hunt was to be our new shining star up front. With the demise of Durham City, The Hunt is now available almost every Saturday and with his past record in the league, we should be comfortable against the weaker teams. Jona has been known to me for years. He's instantly recognisable by having the largest skull in

WHITE SHORTS WHITE SOCKS

North Sunderland. His football skills are excellent. He tends to keep hold of the ball too long, but generally uses it positively. Jona also invented the name Sassco (six a side soccer company). Jeff was also available and, surprisingly, Robason was there as well. Roba's been working on Saturday mornings in a clothes shop in the city centre. I've tried to persuade him to quit so the next option is to send loads of people there to get him the sack.

So, we had a full squad with three subs (including me) and we kicked off, immediately creating an impact on a disaster of a pitch. The referee, who seemed spaced out, missed some dubious decisions and Wardle stole in to score the opener. Most of the first half was spent camped in their area, but our final ball was diabolical. We eased the pressure off the team by slagging off Muers for all the game and I was close to switching Muers and Dixon for the second half, just so we could continue our tirade against the balding winger. Wardle eventually grabbed a second after coming close on occasions. The opposition was weak, and I'm really disappointed we didn't get more.

At half time, I pulled off Wardle and Jeff to put on Kelsey and Hunt. The game was over at 2-0. We were far too comfortable and Robason, who played almost unnoticed, won everything thrown at him. It was good to have a solid centre half. First time since Paul Mouat and Mav used to play for us. Harper, for all his sins, played well. He was immobile as his pace from his small legs isn't really up to the high standards, we expect of him. He combined well with his arch nemesis, the Hutt and was unlucky not to score, with a header cannoning off the post. But with the Hunt on, we gained a penalty which Mark Muers took and missed. Work this one out - we've had two penalties in two years and Muers has taken and missed both. So, he was the obvious choice then. But luckily It wasn't too long after when he did score to make it 3-0. Harper then threw one of his famous wobblers and launched into a red faced, albino haired opposition player. He got a yellow card for it and his aggression was much welcome. Gash also had a blinder in centre mid. He got stuck in and gave 100% which all bodes well for the final on Wednesday.

WHITE SHORTS WHITE SOCKS

Defeated in the Final - 12th February 2004

It's difficult not to be disappointed. At the start of the competition, we were clear favourites. We had a genuinely good side. We beat Low Fell 4-0 away in our peak at the start of the season. Times change but I still managed to put out a very good and well-balanced team out there.

It started well, the whole day did. The team was there early, and we had a full complement, like we did on Saturday. Kelsey, Stubbs and Jeff Clark were nominated substitutes, and the only selection dilemma was if Jase was to be centre half or Booth. In the event, Jase started as centre half and Booth played there in the second. Emu and Wardle up front, Stapes on the left, Digga on the right. Gash and Greenwell in the middle. Robason, Jase as centre halves. Booth right back and Galey left back. A good all-round team.

But during the game, once we went a goal down, the

facts were plain. Where it counted, we didn't deliver. Up front we simply didn't create a chance or an opportunity. Both Wardle and Muers wanted it on a plate and simply couldn't fashion an opening against a very immobile defence. The midfield quartet of Greenwell, Staples, Brazier and Dixon completely failed in winning the ball. Staples did himself justice to an extent, but his passing was diabolical. Dixon was too far inside instead of pulling out wide and creating more space. We should have scored first. Muers came close when his slow shot just shaved the post. No one followed up though. And dragging shots wide or off target isn't good enough. We must take our chances.

The defence didn't really have a great deal of problems apart from creating problems themselves. An inability to clear the ball was married with Low Fells inability to take advantage. Robason was a star, but like

I said in the team talk, it wasn't going to be a game where the defence would be under pressure. But even then, we caused ourselves problems. Galey, I'm sure was just trying to impress the lasses. Watson made some stunning one on one stops to keep us in it, but like I said in few match reports a while back. It's no point Watty keeping us in the game when the strikers are simply nothing short of impotent.

WHITE SHORTS WHITE SOCKS

The only goal of the game came when the team failed to stop a cross coming in and failed to pick up their hulking forward who made no mistake. The goal was early and gave us ample opportunity to respond – but we didn't.

At half time I made a switch. Greenwell was injured, so Jeff came in as centre midfield alongside Gash. Dixon was replaced by Kelsey. We had 45 minutes to do it and we didn't. Well pissed off with Muers and Wardle. The one game where I wanted them to perform, they didn't.

I'm never interested in them scoring goals against mingin teams. We came close in the dying minutes, but I need a team to create chances in the 90 minutes not in the last few. Stubba came on for Jase, and lo and behold, he was the closest in taking the game to extra time.

Bringing in extra players to the squad is welcome now. The likes of John Hunt and Billy Harper, although they probably don't have the pace compared to Muers and Wardle, can create goals and set their own players up – something we were lacking. The lads have got to look at themselves now. The excuse of "at least we got to a final" is bull shit. The competition is naturally weak. We bludgeoned some of our opponents earlier in the cup and in the league, so don't give me any crap about coming second in a weak competition.

WHITE SHORTS WHITE SOCKS

Baker returns - 14th February 2004

Well fuck me senseless. Of all the people in the world, a new and improved Baker turned up. And not only did he turn up, but he also brough a fresh set of £20 notes to pay off his fine. Staggering, truly staggering. Also, the game was taking place on Valentine's Day. The main topic in the changing room was what had Wayne and Wardle got each other. From my understanding, they were due to have a "wonderful" evening together.

And after the disappointing final, I expected a reasonable turn out, instead we got a tremendous turn out. 14 players in total. Greenwell was injured and Jase was working, but apart from that, every regular was there. Including the Tash and Hunt.

The opposition were more than half decent, but our problem seems to be that we view each major opposition in awe. Silks Cath Club are, as a team, far stronger than us, but individually, it's difficult to say players like Wardle, Staples, Baker, etc wouldn't have a problem in fitting into any team.

The set up was reasonably balanced, but with the vast turnout, the team was going to suffer from rotation. I've said it time and time again, if we have regular players paying £2 subs, there's no way they're going to stand on the side-lines. People like Wardle whinge a lot and from a player's perspective its fully understandable, but when the shit hits the fan, it's our hard-core regulars who will always be there: Greenwell, Dixon, Booth, Watty, Staples, Galey etc.

For this game, Dixon, Galey and Harper were benched. Wardle partnered Hunt up front for the first time. Stubbs and Booth were centre halves, but the rest of the team was as normal. Watty, as always was in goal and certainly lost a few pounds after running out early to pick off and cut out problem long balls from the opposition. We created chances and boy did we create them. Gash hit the cross bar and the follow up was launched over the bar. Silks hurtled down the pitch and scored immediately. They were causing no end of problems, and I envisioned a walloping. They soon went 2-0 up, but we grabbed one back. Hunt's good work led to Wardle scoring from a goal mouth scramble. We then turned it on for the remainder of the half. Pressure was applied and silks were scrambling to clear their lines. But as with Sassco throughout this season, we failed to score. We missed 4 gilt-edged, obvious chances and suffered the consequences. Peoples say "at least we create the chances..." But it's no good, simple as that. I'd rather get walloped fair and square with no chances instead of wondering "what if?" after all the chances we missed. I remember Shiney Row at home. Kelsey's mate squandered so many chances in the first half and we lost in the second. I for one will never pat anyone on the back for missing good chances, just the same as I wouldn't pat our defence when then struggle. And Stubba did - playing mainly because Jase wasn't there, Stubba caused a crucial third goal in the second half, instead of clearing his lines, he had the impression that he was a good footballer and tried to play it out. Stubba's monkey DNA didn't kick in and his legs gave way, like they did most of the game. The funniest thing in the first half was Stubba hurtling up the field and losing the ball, then hurtling back and clearing it and then bollocking everyone – brilliant. But this time it wasn't brilliant - it was 3-1 and it was over.

We did have further chances, and most were missed. Dixon came on for Muers and spent most of the time out of position instead of out wide. Simple thing is that if the winger is far out wide, the least that will happen is that he'll take one of their defenders with him. also, his confidence is truly shot to bits. Twice he was in the box and should have shot, but with a lack of confidence, elected to pass instead. Wardle was useless again. I was told he had sciatica, but I couldn't give a fuck what religion he is, he's not performing and more importantly, has not getting his shots on target. Harper came on for Gash and Wardle was pushed deeper, but to be honest, he simply didn't make a difference at all. Playing against teams such as SW Gardens, where he had a blinder is far different to the likes of Silks. But we still allow the opposition to pass the ball around instead of closing every lost cause down – and whenever we do, we always cause problems, but our lost still don't learn and persist with it. Does my head in sometimes.

Jona had an encouraging game and eventually scored from a penalty. We were 5-1 down at the time so it was only a consolation – at least Muers was off the pitch not to take it. But the embarrassing thing was seeing all the players milling around the ball like flies' round shite waiting to take a penalty.

Really disappointed, we need to increase our own confidence and have belief that we are just as good as the other decent teams, we've done it before at the start of this season also the start of last season. And people say to me, give some encouragement. If it's encouragement you want, go and bring your parents to watch you.

Twigs and car parts for net pegs - 21st February 2004

It was going to be one of those fun days again. I was ill so I didn't even bother putting me lenses in, there's no way I wanted to play, but the Studio were the type of opposition I enjoy playing again - not rough, won't get me kit dirty, etc. As for the rest of the team, Baker was ill and absent. Digga was ill but played for a bit, and we had a full squad. The usual bollocks about the nets happened, we used string, twigs, car parts anything, to put them up - the Sassco way. Eventually the growth of bushes and trees behind the pitch will probably vanish as we seem to use a tree a week to hold the nets down. But one has to learn to improvise...during the past two weeks, I've used a straw and an empty tin of ASDA beans to hold the midlife crisis fanny magnet together. I plonked Stubba and Staples on the bench, Stubba for the hell of it and Staples because I thought he wasn't going to play due to injury. The team was reasonably strong; Watty, Booth, Jase, Galey, Kelsey, Gash, Greenwell, Digga and Muers. With Fatty and Hunt up front.

Game wise I'd say the performance was overall disappointing. When playing teams weaker than us, we cannot finish our chances. When we play the strong teams, we won't win if we don't finish our opportunities. We are much better than Studio, but the number of chances we squandered in the first 30 minutes had me tearing my (rapidly greying) hair out and practically pleading with the forwards to score. We did get one in the first. Digga sent a looping ball over to Wardle who chested it down and allowed Muers (Dunston) to steal in and beat four (yes four!) players to send in a perfect shot. I was readying my "pass the ball you bald bastard." when he took on his third man but didn't need it. We'd gone close earlier on. Dunston sent in a perfect corner which Hunt connected on, but it and Wardle had missed a one on one.

By this time, Digga hauled himself off and started to make weird gurgling noises by sitting in the car behind us. Staples made an appearance on the right (at his own request) and the game continued. I still can't believe the number of chances we squandered throughout the game. The pressure was eventually taken off when Wardle scored in the second half. Studio had some glorious opportunities with the long ball over the top and their tall striker (aka Lurch), having some chances. We caused our own problems at the back. For a change, Watty made some mistakes which was refreshing to see. Jase played his usual no nonsense style of launching the ball, and we were taking bets on both him and Kelsey on who'd give a penalty away first. Greenwell and Gash were in the middle, but sometimes struggled to hold their position allowing the opposition to take control in that area. Greenwell nearly got cautioned, but at least he would have had a card on his birthday. Gash spent too much time whinging at the referee instead of playing to the whistle. The referee was okay but gave some abnormal decisions. A Staples shot which the keeper saved and parried for a corner was given as a goal kick! But all due respect to the ref, Harper thought he looked like Rudolf Hess, that's fresh, Harper himself looks like Stalin.

Thankfully Wardle scored a third and decisive goal.

Jona was shattered, he didn't get a goal, but probably didn't deserve one after he missed a true clanger from around 5 yards out. He even tackled Dunston on one occasion but still didn't come close. On one occasion,

WHITE SHORTS WHITE SOCKS

Fatty had me gob smacked. When we were only 1-0 up, he missed a proper clanger. "you're a fat bastard." I told him. He said, "and you're white..." Gob smacked, I didn't even have a wisecrack to reply to him neither. Never mind though, good game. The crack on the side-lines was truly outstanding, makes it all worthwhile. Tash and Anth "the goat" Mouat were there and contributed. Although Anth was again whinging about the team selection, etc. But he soon changed the subject when I told him "That I really couldn't give a fuck about his opinion." Even Tash got frightened off as well, and I for once will never ever take criticism on the Adidas Ball. "It's Adidas, man - it's alright."

Well done to Studio 2000. They themselves contributed to a genuinely entertaining game. I think their lads had a good laugh on the side-lines and on the pitch.

We always have a good game against them. Two 3-3 draws last season. A good strong away win this season and two tight games at home at the start, 3-2 and 2-2.

We still need a sponsor though. At least £400 is needed to continue next season. There's no way me and Boothy are going to put it in and I'm not really going to ask all the lads to contribute. Pitch fees are £240. League entrance fees probably top around £100 and I

WHITE SHORTS WHITE SOCKS

reckon we probably need a new kit at some stage - although the current one is usable. The badges have faded badly so I'll get them done myself.

WHITE SHORTS WHITE SOCKS

Comfortable victory - 20th March 2004

The few weeks off did me and the team the world of good.

Firstly, I managed to erect a fence border around my decking I put down months ago. Absolute top notch and very sturdy, the wife was impressed and so was Wobbly Harper who eagerly asked me for a photo of it. More odd jobs included a new bath panel, a re-constructed Thursday league web site, a new wooden frame around the beloved Sassco photograph (you know...the one taken before we were kebabbed by the Club 6-0).

We were due to play Britannia. I was absent from the game, but it was called off even before a ball had been kicked (or Wayne Greenwell had woken up). So, it was against our old mates, the Geordies who deservedly beat us 1-0 in the Final. Now the thing is that nobody, including myself will give them credit for that win, because we simply didn't fire on all cylinders. A lot of our lads suspected they'd brought in their signed "superstars" for the final, and this suspicion was slightly confirmed when the team they presented had no subs and quite a few unknowns. To me it's sad, and I'm not angry about it. I could have drawn up Paul Mouat, Corby, etc for the final and we would have walked it even before the opening whistle – but I would have never forgiven myself. I remember saying, nearly two years ago, that "we win with this team and no other side." basically saying that the line-up wouldn't really change unless forced and ringers wouldn't be required for any of the major matches. This philosophy of mine hasn't changed and never will. In my opinion, getting something out of team which you don't expect is the best thing. A prime example is our start this season. The win over the Sandhills and the draw against the Daisy was done with just about the same team which suffered so many ignominious defeats last season – that's why those results were so precious.

The only changes from the Cup Final team were the addition of Baker and Hunt, both who missed the Final due to suspension and ineligibility respectively. My team talk was very basic, and this was after we improvised with twigs, car parts, a colourful plastic toy gun and a chair in order to put up the nets. The instructions were to get stuck in and give no quarter. Also, any opposition player with "Spice Boy" hair styles were to be scythed down. Everyone was comfortable with their positions, and it was Gash and Muers on the side-lines. I was very tempted to plonk Digga on the subs bench to start off with but thought "fuck it." he's had a bad run recently and putting him on the bench wouldn't help rectifying it. Lucky for me, my decisions in this game were 100% vindicated and Digga got his first Man-of-the- match award.

Within minutes we were camped in their half. Big Bazza was in goal this time, so they didn't really have a physical threat in attack. Hunt came close to start with and so did Booth. But it was Wardle who opened the scoring. We never looked back. Digga looked good – he was playing as an out and out winger and seemed to be gaining in confidence. He contributed towards the goal and managed to reach the bye-line on several occasions and struck some perfect crosses which caused problems. It was his just rewards when he stole in from the righthand side to score the second goal. It was easy and we were coasting. Boothy had his best game for a while and was unlucky to score (at the opposition end this time). Baker had a blinder. His skill in side-stepping each challenge and releasing the perfect ball was allied to his sheer aggressiveness in "wiping out" the opposition when they had the ball. Each time he went in, he caused problems. He did so by pressuring the opposition and forcing them into mistakes.

The second half saw Low Fell open their account. It didn't last long though. I'd put Muers on for Staples as the little fella had a difficult game. By this time, it was raining hard, and he was in danger of drowning in some of the big puddles now developing in our once lush arena. Muers came on and eventually grabbed a goal as the Low Fell back line opened. I then switched Gash for

Hunt and he scored we a neat back heeler to make it 4-1.

A good comfortable result which was enjoyed by all. We reiterated the need for a sponsor or a large cash injection to continue next season, but time is clearly running out, and like Jona said to me afterwards, it'd be a huge shame it wouldn't go on as the crack is fantastic. I remember the Tash and Tanj deriding me before the start of last season after I told them I was in it for a laugh.

Well chaps, that's what genuinely keeps me going. I don't take it seriously; I don't take myself seriously. I demand more than I really expect from what I've got on the pitch, and they certainly enjoy it now more than they ever have. And the reason is? Because it's a good laugh....

WHITE SHORTS WHITE SOCKS

A hammering - 27th March 2004

Let's stop beating around the bush. Footballers are thick – the whole lot of them. They come into football with little or no education and make it big based on their own abilities. Take Damien Duff for example – by far, one of Chelsea's best players, but in a recent 442 interview he said he doesn't do interviews because he "can't be arsed." The ridiculous 442 interviewer kissed his arse by saying that it was refreshing to hear. Bollocks he can't be arsed because he's thick as pig shit.

I listen to 5 live every day and after the Leicester problems that daft twat Julian Worricker (who spends about a minute spouting shite instead of saying things straight) holds debates (his fave word) about why they do it. Why! Because t-h-e-y a-r-e t-h-i-c-k. Let us take

Stubba as an example, he's barely got 10 pence in his pocket and he's a moron. Put 10 grand in his pocket he's still a moron. There's your typical footballer. The

WHITE SHORTS WHITE SOCKS

Sassco lads get up to all sorts of shit each weekend. Pissed as a fart, shagging owt that moves. You put cash in their pocket, they're still going to do the same.

I think the FA and FIFA should bring in a new rule. Players should not be interviewed unless they have at least 4 GCSE pass grades (C and above). I really detest thick footballers. Rio Ferdinand, thick as pig shit, struggles to string a few sentences together, deserves to be banned for life and condemned because he's thick. Now he has some time off I reckon

he needs to start learning some education.

Oh, and we lost 8-1 or 9-1 against the Sandhills. I'm sure one of the Sandhill's lads shouted over to mention his goal on our website. Most of us were confused – The goat thought he meant building site. Well anyway, we'd be happy to mention it on our website – but would expect a mention for Sassco on the Sandhills website as well. Cola Boy also returned to us for this game. Now there is the genuine metrosexual spice boy. Called "Cola Boy" because he was a rep for Coca Cola, he just upped and left near the end of last season to go travelling. But after spending a year out boning girls (and probably boys) around the world, his tints needed redoing, so he came back to sunny Sunderland to get them done and also play for the team again. He played well when he

WHITE SHORTS WHITE SOCKS

came on.

WHITE SHORTS WHITE SOCKS

Tactics, tactics, tactics - 8th April 2004

"Yaar tactics are all wrong!!" howls the toothless (literally) Greenwell. Tactics? we haven't got any tactics.

The team hasn't got the brains for any tactics. I'll tell you what. I'll sort the tactics and complicated stuff once we've learned how to do the following:

Clear the ball properly.

Win it in midfield - especially when in the air.

Take our chances in attack.

I'll tell you what tactics are. Using the wind to advantage to take long shots. Something which Wardle in all his brains failed to do. The midfield was nothing short of diabolical. Greenwell for all his whinging didn't win a single 50-50 in the air when he was contested by their opposition player and hasn't done all season. Hollymere were terrible and so were we. But they took advantage of our mistakes whereas we simply didn't

WHITE SHORTS WHITE SOCKS

have the brains to do anything about it. Even the normally reliable Robason looked shaky - but that was probably the fact that eventually we've dragged him down to our level. Jase kept slicing his clearances, Boothy looked nervous and Gash as centre half simply didn't work. I'll probably try him there again as he's one of the only ones who wants to play there.

Midfield was shite. Baker turned up looking like someone off the Black and White Minstrels show and played the same - toothless. And Greenwell - he's holding the most important role in the team and simply isn't delivering the goods. I think we've been papering over the cracks by commending his aggression, but when the balls in the air - like it always is, we can't compete. It all came to bare on the Sandhills game when a clearly overconfident and unfit Cola Boy cancelled out the opposition player who was winning the ball all the time.

And upfront - Jona was the only outstanding player along with Watty (as always) in goal. Stapes, Muers and Digga didn't do much, although Muers did add some fun to the proceedings. Galey, Stubba and Muers came on in the second half and probably Galey did the most out of all of them. Stubba went on one of his runs and lost the ball (and a goal). Muers just meandered around.

WHITE SHORTS WHITE SOCKS

We started extremely fragile. The opposition had around 6 corners on the trot but were too shite to do anything with them. We wanted to see how many times we could pass the ball in the opposition box as well. And every time we cleared the ball, we didn't win it, despite me saying in the team talk that we needed to win when we clear it. Again, it points to midfield – a ball in the air is a ball lost. Jona scored both our goals when we were 2-0 down. The first was a superb penalty won by Staples and the second was a pile driver from the edge of the box.

We should have gone 3-2 up. Jona, again in the thick of things, saw his shot rebound off the keeper and fall in the path of Wardle – who missed. Fucking moron. They scored immediately after that and eventually went 5-2 up.

So, we're running out of competitions to get knocked out of. On Saturday we've got the bloody Daisy again.

Getting sick. Isn't there any shite teams left in the league (apart from us)? Getting sick of getting walloped.

So, losing 5-2 was embarrassing and instead of worrying about tactics, we have to learn our basic passing, clearing, winning the ball and taking shots and our chances. Then we'll move on to more complicated

WHITE SHORTS WHITE SOCKS

systems such as joined up writing and Mr. Men books.

4-4 draw - 10th April 2004

Sassco really baffle me sometimes. The same team which got walloped off Sandhills and beaten by Hollymere turned out against an ominously dangerous looking Mountain Daisy team. The bad blood emanating from the earlier game which saw DFA act against Daisy for racism was still there.

Ironically, they got off after making an appeal. It was essentially my word against theirs – and they did have "their" referee on their side as well. But then again, it's not the first time I'll be called a racial slur, and it certainly won't be the last time. Speaking from a truly independent point of view, it's no wonder why there's so much strife between the Asian and black communities and the white communities now because of crap like this. Most older Asians and blacks don't really trust anyone anymore due to the harsh treatment they got in the 70's and 80's. I for one can still remember racism vividly in West Yorkshire in the 70's and 80's. NF marches. Posters going up with "official nigger targets". My old man telling me about his bus being pelted with eggs when he was a bus driver. Me and my old man being racially abused when I must have only been around five or six years old when using a public toilet by another bloke. So, when all throw their arms up in anger that the "foreigners" don't integrate into society – well they'll know now why. There's still too much bad blood and memories. I was bornin the UK and fully bred there. I don't have any single Asian person as a friend and only hang around with white people as I have all my life. I also hate religion and am a devout atheist. I also don't agree with the notion of asylum neither, but I for one won't hoist up the Union Jack and start singing "hallelujah" until all racism has ended (which it won't).

Back to the game. As I said it was ominous. The whole Daisy team were geeing their own team up against a silent Sassco team before the opening whistle, and it worked. We were swamped in the first twenty minutes, and it seemed that Daisy would bang one in sooner rather than later. Strangely, when we broke, we simply sliced through the Daisy back line. Staples fired over the bar with the goal at his mercy. The confidence immediately rippled through the team. We had a forward line of Hunt and Wardle and a new midfield of Jeff partnering Baker in the middle. Stapes and Muers were on the flanks while a brave decision (I may say) by myself prompted by Greenwell put him in the centre half position. Gash, who had a nightmare in the same position on Wednesday, also remained in that position. This was a key area and luckily for me – it worked. Both were truly outstanding. Jase was left back and Boothy was right back and both had outstanding games. Jase, again, looked nervous as left back on Wednesday, but today, looks as if he's played there all his life. Stubba held the goal and was sure as hell in catching the ball and commanding his area.

But the good performance was given a setback with around two minutes until half time. Daisy grabbed one off a set piece free kick, but our heads clearly weren't down. Half time talk was simple and to the point "keep at it." I took Stapes off at his own request due to injury and plonked Jeff on the wing. He was replaced in the middle by Cola Boy. Jeff looked forlorn in midfield and failed to make an impact. Cola Boy did the opposite.

Mountain Daisy's key player is probably Mark Gibson (who also turned his six-a-side team, Ellie Leisure's season around when he started for them in the Tuesday league). He was running the show and causing no ends of problems. Cola Boy stuck tight on him and won most of the high balls (mainly due to his height advantage). But he also riled Gibson up – not surprising really, our lot want to kick Cola Boy's head in most of the time as well. But Gibson lost his strength in his game and concentrated on lynching the Cola Boy instead. The whole Daisy team were far more aggressive in the game, but we matched them in the response. Especially from the Cola Boy.

Obviously, he wouldn't win a fight against any of the opposition, but it wasn't about fighting, but about gaining the upper hand in tactical terms. More and more fouls were being given against him and it was obvious that we broke up their play in the second half. So, it wasn't really surprising that we scored. Cola Boy began the move which ended with Muers lashing it in. Muers had a good solid game. His work rate was still low, but he caused them problems. At one occasion Daisy were saying "get him out of the game." Little do they know; he usually does that himself. Wardle is still not firing on all cylinders. Even during our dark days last season, he still came in with some stunners from distance. In this game, he barely had a shot and was snipered on regular occasions. The opposite must be said for Hunt. His presence was strong, and his one liners were even better (although he got a yellow card for it). Baker had a quiet but effective game. He rarely gave away a pass which is so crucial for us as every second of possession is so crucial. We came close on so many occasions after this and were very disappointed to be ending the game on level terms. Extra time didn't open neither. We did have glimpses of chances, but passes were astray as the team got tired. Kelsey was on now for Jeff as the team went into the penalty shoot-out. Openers from Wardle and Cola Boy were taken comfortably, but both Jase and Jona missed to send us out. Both of theirs hit the upright and post. Never mind. I forgot to mention (obvious now though) that this was a cup game in a league which seems to have more cups than Mario Kart.

And to go back to the opening statement. Sassco still baffle me. This result reminds me exactly of the last game of last season away to the Cliff. I made positional changes after a string of bad results, and we gained an impressive win. More importantly, we built on it. We had a narrow 3-2 loss against Durham in the friendly and then had a storming season opener which included 8-3 wins away to Hollymere and a 5-1 win over Sandhills. Ironically this culminated in a 4-4 draw with the Daisy when we were 4-2 down. After this we thought we were invincible and haven't recovered since. Despite all this rhetoric, we still lost against the Daisy on penalties. But to me, to take it so far and have a good solid performance means so much. In my eyes we didn't lose but drew and we've got to take something from that and build on it. If we don't, then it's classed as another Sassco day – when we pull out all the stops and play well, but don't bother the next week.

WHITE SHORTS WHITE SOCKS

Daisy again - 17th April 2004

Match report by Michael Booth.

With Dov at work, I was left to rally the troops as Sassco entertained Daisy for the second consecutive Saturday, this time in the Quarter Final of the Sangha cup. The team lined up with Watson replacing Stubba in goal, back four (Booth, Gash, Greenwell and Jase), midfield (Dixon, Baker, Jeff and Muers) and Wardle and Hunt leading the attack. The game was refereed by Muers best friend Mr Gordon, who had sent off 4 of our players this season for dissent. The first half continued from last week with both teams seeming to cancel each other out. Daisy, however, took one of their few chances after poor marking from a set-piece let them in for the opener. With half-time approaching Sassco had their best chance of the game, Hunt strolled past the Daisy defence and rocketed a shot off the crossbar, re- bounce fell to Wardle (who is on a bit of a barren spell at the moment) and his shot was well saved and then Muers should have done better from the loose ball.

Half time 1-0 to the Daisy. Dixon was replaced with Galey. Told Stubba he would be on in about 5 minutes as he had to get Dixon's kit off him. With the score still 1-0 the swine entered the fray replacing myself. I thought I would try to use my managerial skills standing on the touchline. Daisy soon doubled their advantage after a mix-up between Stubba and Watson. Watson seemed to have the ball safely in his hands, but it squirmed loose leaving an easy tap-in after Stubba had knocked him for 6 (after a push from a Daisy player).

What would Sassco's response be, heads normally start to drop. Hunt responded smashing the ball off the underside of the crossbar once again. Gash was fouled trying to get the follow-up. PENALTY!!! Hunt decided to take the responsibility, you could hear the Daisy lads saying, "He'll miss, he'll miss he did last week" and sure enough he blazed his penalty high over the bar. (A penalty Johnny Wilkinson would have been proud off). But at least he had the guts to take it.

Time was running out, the only player I had available to try and turn the game around was Kelsey as Staples was injured. Jeff was whinging saying he wanted to come off and calling the team "useless", but Kelsey preferred to stay on the touchlines and laugh at Jeff. Muers moved further up field to partner Hunt and Wardle, but this seemed to confuse Wardle and he dropped further back. Currently Stubba was doing his famous bursts up field without the ball. Daisy introduced a tall striker who sewed up the win for the Daisy and ended Sassco's final cup run of the season with 2 strikes in the last 5 minutes, one from a 20-yard free kick.

No subs collected from several team-members including Stubba once again. When will he realise, we need money to survive as a team?

Note from Davinder: don't worry. I'll send a letter to DFA like I did last time to force Stubba to put his hand in his pocket…simian twat!! Also, I wasn't at work, just felt like some time off.

WHITE SHORTS WHITE SOCKS

Dixon turns up in a suit - 21st April 2004

A typical away day. Bad organisation, lack of shirts, fatty turning up in blue shorts. There were changes in the team, most we forced changes. Gash was missing (work) so Stubba (with £2) slotted in as centre half with Wayne (kicked out of his house). Jase was left back, and Booth was right back. Kelsey came in as right winger (both politically and positional) as Galey (gammy foot) and Staples (gammy toe) were out. Jeff was missing due to work (liar) and kept a top with him. It baffles me why any player should take a shirt home with him when he cannot commit to Wednesday and Saturday games. Simply not acceptable. Cola Boy was also missing (having his highlights done). So, I popped Digga and Hunt up front and (asking for trouble) Fatty with Baker in the middle.

For the first time I employed a small tactic as now the team seems to have moved on from joined up writing and now on to pushing different shaped blocks into the correct holes. I've always identified the Clubs backline on being slow. They hold an excellent offside trap and are very physical. But Digga was to stay on the last man and break at every opportunity. The plan seemed to work but eventually we didn't take advantage of it.

It almost didn't happen. Digga was late, but he did tell me he was going to be. Kelsey and Hunt were holed up in the changing rooms having a chat and a cup of tea. So, we nearly started with 8 players. We did start with 10. Digga turned up looking like Neo off the Matrix and had to take his suit tie, cufflinks, etc off to get ready. But it did give me an opportunity to give him instructions. Also, the team got on his back to hurry up, so by the time he was on the pitch, he was well pissed off.

Performance was good overall. For the third consecutive game, the defence was solid. Unfortunate lapses led to their two opening goals. Both came from our left-hand side. A simple cross (which wasn't prevented) and a header in. We were clearly disappointed, but it didn't affect the performance. Both Hunt and Dixon came close. Dixon should have scored when clear on. Wardle also came close but simply failed

WHITE SHORTS WHITE SOCKS

to deliver in the middle like he always doesn't. Now I could have plonked Greenwell in the middle, but it would have cancelled out the defence which is the only thing which looks good in the team. Kelsey played well but seemed to be intimidated by the opposition - Kelsey scored in our last game here. Muers, after a good first half, died in the second and got into difficulties. The only major chances in the second were a shot from Baker on his weak left foot and clanger from Muers. Wardle also failed to take advantage of the slope on the field and was useless like he has been in his last three games. Hunt was excellent as always; he threw himself about and caused problems.

The thing about Hunt is that if he isn't scoring, he's getting stuck in so regardless of the result he always gives his all. The only other player on the team like that is probably Staples. Jase, Greenwell, Stubba and Booth were all solid. Greenwell stumbled to cause one goal, but apart from that it was an impeccable performance. Jase's clearances and anticipation were also good. Stubba slotted well as centre half instead of Gash and Boothy's forward play was quite good as well.

But as with the last three games (including this one), we aren't scoring and the longer a game goes on, the more goals we'll concede - not out of bad defending, but the fact that the opposition have the confidence with a goal and also the fact that we're pushing up.

Gourlay returns - 6th May 2004

I expected another dodgy day. In our last game against South Shields, we were very short of staff. Stapes, Cola Boy, Wayne, Jase, Digga, Galey were all missing. Stapes and Cola Boy, I knew about. Cola turned up to pay his fine wearing standard student attire (i.e. flip flops) and was tempted to play, even though he looked comatose.

Jase was missing completely, and I couldn't get hold of him. Wardle surprisingly managed to get hold of

WHITE SHORTS WHITE SOCKS

Jeff's kit. Wayne was missing completely as well. Digga turned up to drop his kit off (and this time he wasn't dressed like Neo off the Matrix like he was on Wednesday). Gourlay rang me the night before asking what time we were on to watch, but I told him to bring his boots - good choice as well, as he made a comeback.

He grabbed two goals in a very enjoyable end of season performance. We had a line-up of Watty in goal, Boothy, Gash, Stubba and me (yes me!) at the back. Fatty, Baker, Kelsey and Dunston were in midfield and Gourlay joined up around five minutes after kick-off to partner Jona in attack. We went 1-0 down after a mix up but soon took advantage of our dominance. Kelsey grabbed the all-important equaliser with an assist from Gourlay and we never looked back. Muers scored an unusual goal which almost looked like it went behind the goal and back in. Probably the horrendous way we set the nets up. The pitch had been cut and cleaned up, so we didn't have any car parts. Although I did use some seat springs in an innovative manner.

The second half saw Jona score and Wardle score (finally). A long-range effort which was perfect as it looped over the 'keeper. Forgetting the positives, we let two easy goals in. Boothy blames himself for one and I blame him for the other. Kelsey was chasing the midfielder (who looked like Dixon with long hair), and the ball overran, which meant Boothy had it, but he didn't, and they scored. This was the reason why he missed two scorchers in the last two minutes. The first one glanced the crossbar and that was it. But amazingly, he got a second chance a few minutes later but walloped it against the post. Obviously if he went to church on a regular basis and was generally a good person, he would have had one in the bag, like I did on the six-a-side on Thursday evening (my first ever competitive goal!) Positive day, nice day, great weather and everyone up for it. We also agreed that a one off £25 is to be paid by all to keep us in the league and a regular £10 at the start of each month instead of paying subs now. There was some disagreement over if someone paid and then was injured, but it was easy to work that out by either refunding the amount or carrying it over to the next month. The reason for the

£10 is simple. It's now the players who pay's responsibility to be there. I'm quite sure that, for example, Wayne would have been there if he'd paid £10 at the start of the month. Also, when we are short, we cannot guarantee any payments for people we bring in for the last minute. Also, the £25 rule applies to all - if anyone says (on the 1st of June when it's due) that they don't have it, then the lads who have paid will get their

WHITE SHORTS WHITE SOCKS

£25 back and we won't be entering on Saturday mornings. It's down to player power. Also, Keith Brazier has turned down the chance to coach the team. He was very tempted, but I blew it by saying he has to make Muers and Stubba better players. I wanted Keith to do the team talks, etc while I would concentrate on picking the team and organising the day. However, he said he much preferred the "crack" on the side-lines and the day out.

Also, the league has taken offence to all the fucking swearing on my website. The site is my own personal fucking blag to everyone and I can basically write what I fucking want. Free speech anyone? They have reported us to Durham FA for the website as they assume it brings their own league into disrepute. Well, I'd be happy to wave my shiny arse to that. The real reason is that they simply don't want anymore "ethnic" problems like they have had before. I was going to put a complaint in about every single racist comment made at every game after the problems during the Daisy game. They obviously bottled it and wanted it swept under the carpet. The easiest way to get rid was by sending it to Durham who would fine us extensively, thus bankrupting the team – clever stuff. It seems very ironic that when I made a complaint to the league about the racist abuse from Daisy, they washed their hands of it

WHITE SHORTS WHITE SOCKS

and said, "send it to Durham." Pretty amazing how they see a few fucking cunt bollocks swear words and seem to have gone out of their way to do something about it.

WHITE SHORTS WHITE SOCKS

What's the first rule for a manager arranging a squad?

If you want 12 players, make sure 13 are there. If you want a squad of 13 make sure you have 14.

The clanger this time was Cola Boy dropping me in it (work). Luckily, I'd already decided to call up two replacements, the returning McNerney and the Tash. Phil McNerney played for us at the start of last season, but like Cola Boy, he upped and went on a charity drive from the UK to Korea. He then spent the rest of the time in China. So, it was going to be a welcome return. Everything was running smoothly so far. Gash was getting a jiffy on by saying we needed at least one sub, while I responded by saying I'd jammed T-Mobile's communications with the number of texts I'd sent over the last week or so. We were playing a long arranged 11-a-side friendly against O'Neills, but the team was truly decimated due to an important night for the six-a-side at

WHITE SHORTS WHITE SOCKS

Downhill.

We got a squad together and all, but McNerney was making his own way there, but lo and fucking behold, I got a text from him saying he's waiting at the Downhill gates. Now call me a cynical twat, but I reckon somehow, he got Herrington mixed up with Downhill. Simple really Shanghai and Beijing are all but the same. Despite being back for a few weeks now, I reckon he's still suffering jet lag. So, the time was 5:40 and I put the Magnet into full use and got to Downhill within 10 minutes. McNerney told me that we shouldn't expect much from him as he'd been out of action a while, but by God I expected something now having raced down the Washington highway pretending to be James Pond.

Tash turned up slightly late, but to my surprise, everyone was there and ready. Nerney and Jiff were attacking. Stapes and Digga on the flanks. Gourlay and Gash were in centre midfield. I wanted the Tash in centre mid, but his jaw and arse dropped when I told him so defence it was for him. Jase was with him and Jeff on the left and me on the right.

We scored from our first attack. Jiff stole in and megged the keeper with ease. By this time, the Tash had been snipered twice. The bad thing wasn't him being snipered, but the fact that the whole team saw it twice.

WHITE SHORTS WHITE SOCKS

Anyway, they scored from a defensive cock up. I'm sure the Tash was involved, but I couldn't really see as I was hogging the touchline keeping out of the way of the hard football (blown up by Watty no less). We then scored a superb goal set up by me. Under pressure, I connected with the ball during a melee and caressed it towards McNerney, who superbly chipped the 'keeper. A delightful goal created in India and finished in China. But most who saw it would probably say that I just wellied the ball out of defence and McNerney did the dirty work.

They then equalised when we decided to play the offside trap. It was 2-2 at half time and we were comfortable and expected to finish them off in the second period.

Amazingly, no one scored. We kept the same shape and had some chances on goal, but so did O'Neills. They probably came closer with more attacking possession, but the end product wasn't there. Some superb crosses came in, but we seemed to deal with them. The hard pitch also took its toll. Stapes was injured, Digga (sponsored by Bukta) was trying on different pairs of boots every other stoppage and Gash wandered off injured. We held on to be happy with a draw.

WHITE SHORTS WHITE SOCKS

I was pleased and I think most of the lads had a good day out. Gourlay did quite well in the second half and so did Digga. Both dropped deep to help the defence (wonder why they were loitering around where I was standing?). Great to see Phil and the goal he scored. He started slow, but soon got into the swing of things and began to beat players and strike from distance. Jiff was awkward as ever, along with Staples. Gash got stuck in with his centre mid role. Also, in defence, Jase was taking the piss out of himself in front of his work mates by dropping a clanger or two. Harper was genuinely superb as always. Weather was good, opposition were good crack and there were no complaints. The real thing that pleased me was that I managed to get a Sassco team out which was fully capable. Stubba, Wardle, Greenwell, Boothy, Baker, Muers, Kelsey, Hunt, Cola Boy and Galey are all nearly 100% regulars. Any team which lost that number of players would struggle and cancel, but we got the team out and more importantly, they were all Sassco players so at least they knew each other having played in some capacity before.

WHITE SHORTS WHITE SOCKS

Quitting the League - 17th June 2004

As most now seem to know, Sassco 11-a-side will not be taking part in the Tyne & Wear League for next season. There are several reasons for this.

Only three players paid the £25 on the 1st of June. Galey, Watson and Dixon (as expected). The others just came up with an excuse and didn't seem really bothered about paying it on time, despite several warnings. Obviously, the majority of the players don't really give a shit when it really counts.

Boothy has resigned as Team Secretary and General Manager. Reason was the bullshit he kept on getting almost every time he went to the league meetings, which are also amongst the most boring events I have ever been to.

The league has taken offence to all the fucking swearing on this website. This site is my own personal fucking blag to everyone and I can basically write what I fucking want. Free speech anyone? They have reported us to Durham FA for the website as they assume it brings their own league into disrepute. Well I'd be happy to wave my shiny arse to that. The real reason is that they simply don't want anymore "ethnic" problems like they have had before. I was going to put a complaint in about every single racist comment made at every game after the problems during the Daisy game. They obviously bottled it and wanted it swept under the carpet. The easiest way to get rid was by sending it to Durham who would fine us extensively, thus bankrupting the team – clever stuff. It seems very ironic that when I made a complaint to the league about the racist abuse from Daisy, they washed their hands of it and said, "send it to Durham." Pretty amazing how they see a few fucking cunt bollocks swear words and seem to have gone out of their way to do something about it.

I had a cheque for £228 written out and handed into the league to pay up and wipe the slate clean. But when they reported us, the cheque was stopped. I have no intention of putting my hand in my own pocket to pay for a load of bollocks when none of the players want to chip in and the league treats us like shite. All the registered players will have to pay their share of whatever fine comes our way.

WHITE SHORTS WHITE SOCKS

So, it ends. But we shall rise again. Sassco are available for unofficial friendly games with any team. Our home ground will be the 11-a-side astro pitch at Downhill.

WHITE SHORTS WHITE SOCKS

The beginning of the "Lost Year" - 4th July 2004

For once, the problem wasn't getting a team out and ready, the problem was getting there. Somewhere in the vicinity of Killingworth, there is an oasis of pitches. Eventually we found it after directions from the locals. We also made sure that we abused the same locals once they'd given us nice directions. We were close to asking a piss head at one time but though against it. Also, someone needs to explain to David Gourlay that a football pitch is rarely located within a new suburban housing development. Gourlay had McNerney and Digga in his car, Wayne had Wayne, and the rest of us were in

Watty's tank. Surprisingly, Boothy wasn't there because he couldn't be bothered. The invasion had begun.

WHITE SHORTS WHITE SOCKS

NIFC, our opposition, are a multi-cultural team, but were down a few players and had to add two or three lads to their squad. We were missing Jeff, Robason, Muers, Hunt and Kelsey. But we had a solid enough line up.

Personally, I wasn't interested in traipsing all the way to Killingworth and not playing, so I was in. Gash and Greenwell were centre halves, Galey on the right. Middle we had Gourlay and Greenwell. Stapes on the left, Digga on the right and up front, we had Fatty and McNerney.

We outplayed them to be honest with you. We were never in any real danger of losing the game once we kicked off. We were a bit wary though, because some of them were built like brick shit houses. But an early goal from McNerney settled the nerves. Phil eventually scored three, but the highlight of the goals was Stubba's impromptu long-range drive which squeezed in. Wardle also scored and we should have had more. All in all, we were comfortable. Gourlay played exceptionally well, and Gash was also strong in defence and in the tackle. Good game, good outing. Galey and Stapes were given the runaround by one of their players on our left-hand side. I was getting to grips with the game itself (football – you generally kick the ball in the opposite direction).

WHITE SHORTS WHITE SOCKS

Also, must mention the scene where their manager falls on his arse on the side lines. The ref was a yank as well – strange place Newcastle you see.

WHITE SHORTS WHITE SOCKS

Tash, bang, wallop – Part 1 - 18th July 2004

Our normal pre-season game against William Harper's side was still on the calendar despite ourselves not entering any league next season. This was Billy's team based heavily on the Durham Reserves unit, albeit a bit weaker. Last season we suffered a 3-2 loss – anyone remember Dunston's last-minute pile driver saved by Davo? Anyway, we got a lot of credit for that narrow defeat, but for some reason, the key players for Durham seemed to think that it was a flash in the pan our performance. Well, the team's been running for nigh on two and a half years now and each season we always identified weak spots and ironed them out. Put simply,

Tash's minions were no match for a battle hardened Sassco team. We've been unbeaten since our final league game against Britannia. A superb 2-2 draw with a makeshift team (with me and the Tash in defence)

against

O'Neills followed by a strong team winning 5-2 in Killingworth. This time I changed the full backs. Galey, first choice, wasn't there so I called up Kelsey, who wasn't stoned, wasn't pissed and was raring to go. Boothy came back to fill in the right back slot instead of myself. The rest of the line-up was the same, only Jiff came in and I put Fatty on the bench, much to his chagrin, so that Jiff could fill up a fast front line with him and McNerney.

Tash's team comprised of some new faces, but quality players such as McNaught, Hembrough, Barry Cook, Lee Butler and the ever-impressive Turvey (I think that's his name) who turned Dalfest's season around on the Tuesday. Also, in the line-up was Mickey Pearson, who consistently seemed to slag off Sassco at every opportunity last season, despite not really playing for anyone decent. The Tash rates him highly though, so he was at centre back (where he had a mare for us once a couple of seasons ago).

Kick off and immediately we smelled blood. Cross balls were used, and we were being narrowly caught offside or lacked the final killer touch. But it was only a matter of time before we struck. Jiff, playing up front but coming in from the left, struck and the account was open. We had some minor scares. There were goal mouth scrambles, but the defence held superbly. Now if I told the likes of Barry Cook and Lee Butler, the backline for Sassco would be Boothy, Kelsey, Gash and Stubba, I'm sure they'd laugh it off. I probably would. But then again, I've seen them this season and know their stunning ability. Gash and Stubba were nothing short of awesome in the back and kept the shooting on target to a minimum. Watty was also superbly marshalling the team and made certain of most dangerous crosses. Boothy looked extremely comfortable, and Kelsey was just taking the piss. Stapes probably had a quite game, along with Dixon, but Dixon made amends in the later stages. He needs to stick to his position as out and out winger. Midfield was exceptional. The same duo, Greenwell and Gourlay, who played against NIFC, controlled the ball perfectly when they had it. Greenwell was getting stuck in and Gourlay wasn't wasting a single pass. Up front McNerney had an off day. Some of his control was below par, but he made up for it and held the line so well. McNerney will be playing for the Tash next season, and it seemed that he was the one they feared the most – which in turn, took the pressure off Jiff as bagged in the goals.

The second half continued as the first did. Wardle

WHITE SHORTS WHITE SOCKS

was now on, so we had a front four of Jiff, Fatty, McNerney and Dixon – all goal scorers. Excellent play from Wardle led to the second and decisive strike from Dixon. Unstoppable, just like the team. Now we were taking the piss. So many times, we broke through and squandered chances, but eventually one of these led to Mickey Pearson on his arse. He misjudged a long ball and Jiff stole through to give us an unassailable lead. The Tash's team did get one back and I would have expected an upsurge in their team's performance. They got one, but we simply took our next available chance with a hat-trick from Jiff and a 4-1 score line. Outstanding performance from the top down.

I'm sure I'm going to hear it all from the other side about weak line up, etc. Yes, that can be true, but our normal central defensive partnership is usually Robason and Greenwell in competitive games. We also have Galey who's made the left back position his own. I also missed out Jona for this one as well. And also, Muers, for all everyone slags him off. . . well, hang on, you're right, he is actually shite. We'll miss him out of this one.

I got the usual waffle about getting a team back in a league but put your money where your mouth is lads.

And it was, as expected, the ones who didn't bother to pay that made the loudest noise – i.e. Fatty.

WHITE SHORTS WHITE SOCKS

Searing heat - 26th July 2004

When Alfie summoned up the strength to wiggle his arms to signal a sub, my heart sank. We'd began to build a formidable right-side partnership which was coming to fruition only to see it cruelly broken by Haldane's inept second half performance. We were playing our fourth friendly game and this time it was against a strong team in the form of Redhouse FC, run by Dennis Jackson. Sassco having lost so many players summoned "guest" players in the same way you would see guest stars on the

Simpson's. Hembrough and Haldane were the chosen two. Hembrough is superb, small and fast with a keen eye for goal. Haldane is used as a regular referee in my six-a-side league and plays in his own band, Delta 9. Robason also came with them to make his friendly debut. I was playing as well to solidify the back line. Within minutes I was blowing out of my arse due to the searing heat. Dennis Jackson's team were strong. With Hunt, Kelsey and Gash playing for them, there was also Davo in goal, Sheepy (an ex-Sassco player) and Baker. So, it was nearly 50% Sassco. We opened the scoring, and it seemed as if we could pierce them open at will. Criminally we missed so many chances. McNerney had a clanger. Don't know if he's still got his little red book from his mental brain wash in China, but he needs to give himself a good kick up the Karl Marx and get back to the real world. Communism is dead and quite rightly so. The lasses looked like blokes, and the blokes looked like Kelsey. Hembrough, his guest partner missed his own fair share of chances, although Hembrough did finish his set of goals with ease. It was good fun; my feet were dying due to the hard surface and most of the lads were ready to keel over.

In the second half, we should have finished them off. Greenwell missed a sitter from around 6 yards out and that was it. They kept scoring but we kept coming back. Eventually they went two goals ahead in quick succession and we were finished and couldn't summon up the energy to fight back. I would have been happy with a draw, but the defeat was well deserved for Redhouse FC. With Hunt pulling the strings up front, we simply couldn't cope. I haven't got a clue who scored for us. Think Hembrough got three or maybe four. At the other end we seemed to give them away. Indecisiveness led to a couple of goals and the reliance on the offside trap led to another few. Never mind.

Again, the usual words came out from several people that it was a shame we weren't in any league, but ironically Dennis at the opposing end suffered the problems which blighted us in the early stages. Not easy running local football you know.

WHITE SHORTS WHITE SOCKS

Humidity - 29th July 2004

Humid and overcast were the only ways to describe the weather. Pissing it down was a more accurate term just before the half time break. We were playing Si Williamsons Sunday morning team, Lambton, and for once we had a reasonably full strength set up. Si was the guy who runs the complex where we play and is considered a truly outstanding player, with a very scary long throw. For us, Jiff was back and so was Kelsey, after sleeping with the enemy. I was also playing and Mark Sammut, a guy who helps run a team in the six-a-side, came in for a game to help out of the right-hand side.

It was a lively game, and, in the end, we should have won it comfortably. We did go a goal down, but as ever, Jiff equalised and then put us 2-1 ahead. We were controlling the game until Boothy lashed it into the back of the net - his own bleeding net. He's shaved the crossbar, post, etc. on many occasions at the other end during the last two years but seems to be clinical in lashing them past Watty. In the second though, we went 4-2 ahead culminating in a superb individual strike from Greenwell. McNerney had also grabbed one at this stage as we looked sorted. Unfortunately, the opposition made it 4-3 and despite a brief panic, we struck another, so it seemed curtains for Lambton, for whom Si Williamson was clearly pulling their strings. late on they pulled another one back and were on top. As always, we panic even though we're a few goals ahead. Robason gave away the ball immediately on kick off and this resulted in Si equalising. It was with its fair share of controversy as he handled the ball, but referee, Keith Brazier, played on. His shot was perfect as it squeezed in. Miraculously we had an opening, but yes - you guessed it - Little Red Phil was wide with a gaping goal in front of him. I'll tell you something, I bet he never gets a bird pregnant. Unfortunately, it turned sour. Wardle got yellow card which was disappointing as we were all egging Keith to give him a red. He's had a bit of a clanger in these friendly encounters. Basically, he hasn't scored, although when Jiff's on the team, it's so easy to set him up. A simple ball behind the defenders and Jiffs on it like a dot and always beats his man. Sammut played well. His crossing led to some of our goals and his overall play was very good. Everyone else did okay as well. Kelsey was quiet but solid. Stubba and Greenwell and Wardle spent all day arguing with each other. Robason was calm as always in a vain attempt to keep everyone's heads up. McNerney had a good one but missed too many chances or rather, opportunities. Watty was strong in goal, especially when faced with Si's long, bullet throws. I personally did okay as well. I got stuck in and won some crucial balls. Amazingly I can easily last 90 minutes which superb athletes like Alfie (who I've always looked up to) can't seem to do.

Apparently, this could be the last of our full-strength team turning out as most of the lads have their own sides to worry about no. Wardle and co will be outing for the New Demi, while Kelsey and co will be playing for Dennis Jackson's Redhouse team. But we'll persevere. Harper's been harping on about a re-match, which I'll happily entertain, but I don't think the strongest side will be out. Looks like another phone call to Holly and Alfie.

Oxygen anyone?

WHITE SHORTS WHITE SOCKS

Tash, bang, wallop – Part 2 - 5th August 2004

When I came on to replace Dixon just before half time to inspire a superb second half comeback. For William Harper, the obsessed Sunderland North Manager, it was the equivalent of chopping off his own dick and then getting it rammed up his own arse.

There isn't a great deal to say, but I'll try and milk it for all it's worth. Old Tash thought the 4-1 win was a flash in the pan and was obsessed with a rematch. I reluctantly agreed and this time it was the Tash who had the full-strength team out, while I was looking for players. Luckily, we had well enough, with only me as the sub and Gash as a ten-minute hero. You couldn't see a more contrasting set of ideologies. At 7:05pm, there were only four of us in the changing room. By the time we got on the pitch, the Tash FC team was limbering up by professionally warming up. Us lot were stubbing out old tabs and lighting new ones. Also, for the first time, Muers made his friendly debut which was basically asking for it. Also, the Stubba / Kelsey confrontation was on hold. Until after the encounter. I needed all my boys fit and ready to go.

Tash's confidence really put the shits up me as he was ultra-convinced his team wouldn't fail this time. He had a changed forward line up and two decent centre halves.

But, despite a more promising opening half for them, we erupted. A goal scored was probably my fault by bunging Digga out of position as right back! I eventually switched Muers back there once Digga walked off at his own accord. Too much holiday booze had taken its toll on him. I had to come on and if there's one game I wanted my full team out, it was this one. Me coming on didn't bode well at all. But that's where the fun began.

In the second we scored two quick goals to take a 2-1 lead. They equalised and then we just fired up for more. 6-3 was the final score line. Muers, Wardle, Jiff, Greenwell scored, and Red Phil got two. We certainly should have had loads more. Jiff shaved the crossbar on occasions and played a true blinder. Wardle looked increasingly comfortable in the second half with Greenwell, and in my opinion, for the first ever time in two years, played excellent in centre mid. Stapes seemingly won all the high balls. Muers had a better second than a first (that's a compliment). Nerney, again, had a slow start but tortured them in the second. Stubba and Roba were absolute rocks at the back. It showed the dominance considering that when Barry Cook scored their third goal, Stubba was on the wing dragged out of position. Digga had a mare but should have stayed on when I switched him back to right wing. Kelsey didn't come under any pressure and only went off late with a bad back to be replaced by Gash. Watty was comfortable in goal as well. He punched several times much to some peoples' criticism, but having been in goal, the punch is much better than grabbing it and possibly losing it. Well done to all lads. Proud of you all.

There are differing ways to look at this game from a third person's perspective.

The first is Tash's obsession to beat my team. He still hasn't given us any credit and the first thing I heard was that "we never slaughtered them!" We're running out of fixture slots. How many more times do Sunderland North need to be lashed. Now he was there at the start when we were muppets and lost 8-1. We've also had ups and downs over the last two seasons, but the most important thing is that we seem to know where our positions are. We are a very good unit and the team spirit is second to none. This is brought about by me fully controlling the team and not allowing any prima donnas in. Everyone knows the score in the side. Everyone turns up with full subs and fully kitted and always fully up for it.

Secondly. Tash panicked and changed his team too much. The original line up, in my opinion had a good shape to it. A direct comparison is that from our 8-1 two years ago, Watty, me, Wardle, Greenwell, Dixon, Muers, McNerney and Gourlay were all there and still form the bulk of the team. A little over a year ago, the team which lost 15-1 to Mountain Daisy included, Watty, Roba, Kelsey, Stapes, Greenwell, Wardle, Digga, Muers and

Stubba (and me). Keep with the line-up – don't panic over one result. Hembrough is wasted at the back. He "guested" for us against Dennis Jackson's team and scored four goals and should have had more – say no more. They need proper pace up front. The tall lad on my side of the pitch should have probably been up front. I always bung the likes of McNerney, Jiff and Digga up front simply for their pace.

Also, finally, respect. For some reason, the opposition simply won't give us any respect. Strange really. If I ask anyone what they think of the likes of Wardle, Greenwell, Stapes, Jiff, McNerney, Watson and Roba, etc (note – no Muers). The response would be very favourable. So just because it's me running a team, doesn't make them collectively shite. And remember, I played a half and a bit and felt very comfortable.

A great win, without a goalkeeper - 8th August 2004

Without Wardle and co, and more importantly, without Watty in goal, Sassco were under pressure to get a team out against Wavendon. I managed to get Chris Johnson from a team in the six-a-side in goal, at least for the first half. And after Tash dropped us in it, we dragged another guy, Lee Melia, off the streets to play. Apart from that, the team wasn't too different. We had Jase returning for the first time since the O'Neills friendly game and Ryan McNaught, a lad who plays in the six-a-side, as well as for the Tash, came in to play for a winning team for a change.

Wavendon had shit loads of players. They must have had at least five or six subs and in the searing heat I expected them to come out on top. Like all Sassco games, we started slowly as Wavendon had quite a lot of the play. Chris Johnson made some good stops and defensively we were reasonably strong. We went a goal ahead when a miss-hit Muers cross crept into the top corner. 1-0 up and just before the half ended, we gained a second. This time from the spot. Muers scored to give us a handsome 2-0 lead.

The second saw Chris having to leave early, and Dave G, turning up to watch (wearing glasses, etc) was persuaded to go in goal. It was the second half where I expected the team to suffer and concede goals. We certainly did concede but scored plenty at the other end. We went 4-0 at one stage before Wavendon made their inevitable comeback. They were up to 4-3 at one stage before Muers made it 5-4. Wavendon scored again, but that was their last. The final score was 7-4. McNerney helped himself to two goals, while Greenwell and Digga got the others. Muers' hat- trick still baffles us all.

Not bad though - this was a line up without Wardle, Stubba, Robason, Boothy, Watty, Kelsey and Jiff. So, the result was even more surprising. I was slagged off a bit by playing a few players onside, but the morons who shout "offside" should consider looking along the line before shouting it like a bunch of tits. Also, defence was being slagged off by the midfield, when it was the midfield losing it and then expecting someone else to pick up the pieces. No matter.

WHITE SHORTS WHITE SOCKS

It seems as if we'll be entering the Combination league next season or maybe this season if a team drops out.

WHITE SHORTS WHITE SOCKS

Another win - 19th August 2004

In increasingly humid weather conditions, we took on Wavendon again, on a Thursday night. The team was as normal, but with Chris Middlemiss, my co-manager on the six-a-side, guest starring for us. As with all added players, he had a good game and came away with a hattrick. First half,

We were under the cosh for most of the first but managed to squeeze a couple of goals in reply. Minnie grabbed the reply while Greenwell hit a speculative shot which their keeper let through. However, they did gain the upper and it was 3-2 to them at half time.

In the second we improved vastly and gained a goal advantage. At 5-4 we had three gilt edge chances, Digga Greenwell and Minnie all missed good opportunities and they equalised at the end. As mentioned, Minnie grabbed himself a hat-trick, but the highlight was probably Wayne's goal from Digga's corner. This was the first time in two years that we looked dangerous in taking a corner. Greenwell also had a cracking shot against the post from a free kick.

It really began to piss down when Si came on for injured Gash. Then Gash came back on for injured me - then I came back on for injured Wayne. Good laugh though. Ironically this was a strong outfit we had out, far stronger than the previous one which beat the Wavendon.

But it was balanced more as that was Wavendon's first game this season.

The reason it's expensive for normal people to play football - 22nd August 2004

I've been heavily criticised on the message board for letting Sassco fall into debt. But the facts are plain, also just because I wash the kit and make a few phone calls to get the players ready doesn't mean I'm going to pay the bills. If I or Boothy walked, the team would instantly collapse – and that's a fact.

In our first season we had to shell out on kit etc. as well as the league. Also, the team was in disarray with players not paying subs etc. but we were clear at the end of the season. Why? Because the league fees were reasonable.

This season the league screwed up and decided to double the monthlies. This screwed us badly as we don't really have a proper sponsor. So Sassco team owed the league £224 in total. This would mean around 11 players (inc. myself) being asked to pay £20 to the league to pay it off. This would go to Durham FA. We would be suspended until we actually paid the amount off.

What irks me is that the league has put their own fines of £100 resignation fee, £34 forfeit fee and

£75 entrance fee for next season on top of this amount owed. These are basically their own fines. This I am going to appeal against. We finished our fixtures and were free to leave the league. Also charging us £75 for "entering" next season is laughable. This is simply a way of a bankrupt league making more money for themselves. Remember, these are the people who doubled their charges halfway through last season to pay for their bad management.

The only reason I'm holding back on entering the WCFL league is that all the lads would chip in around £25, I'd pay the league fees of £80 + £120 pitch fees and also DFA fees of around £50 then see half the team hit with a suspension just in case it doesn't get appealed and reduced. If all the lads were hit with a £20 fine, then that isn't a problem. If they get hit with £40 then that's a bit more difficult.

WHITE SHORTS WHITE SOCKS

Defeating an African XI - 26th September 2004

Another game against NIFC was hastily scheduled after all the slack arse shits wouldn't put their hands in their pockets to pay for Paintball. This time we had a minor struggle with players. Gourlay was injured but was press ganged into coming along due to us only having 11.

Sammut didn't even turn up after the 1pm phone call was diverted to voicemail (always a sign that someone aint turning up). Boothy is still under the thumb and Digga was apparently hoying up during the Great North Run. So, Minnie got the call up and did his duty.

Team was reasonably strong. Watty, as ever, in goal. Gourlay, Gash, Stubba and me along the backline. Stapes, Greenwell, Wardle and Jeff in the middle and up front, the increasingly shite Dunston and Minnie.

WHITE SHORTS WHITE SOCKS

NIFC really wanted to beat us this time, and they probably had a better chance of doing it. Last time, we had Nerney on form along with an uninjured Gourlay as well as Galey playing. This time we were out of sorts. The first half was hit and miss. With Dunston, inexplicably, missing from around a centimetre out.

Don't ask me how, but there was more chance of me swearing at the ball, and it going in as opposed to Dunston scoring. He spent most of the first half playing "keepy up" before getting bludgeoned off the ball by a huge West African player. Anyway, we did score, and it was Minnie who did the good work from Jeff and Greenwell. We conceded though, around five minutes before half time. One of their lads ran through and lashed the ball past a hapless Nutmeg. Despite this, we should have been ahead. Dunston kept missing and Greenwell was unlucky after he beat around four players only to see his shot squirm wide.

Second half started diabolically. We were being tortured and it was surprising that we didn't concede. Watty made some cracking stops, coming mainly from one-on-ones. Eventually the deadly decision had to be made. Dunston was killing us up front and had to be palmed off to the right wing. Jeff was placed in centre mid, and Fatty was plonked up front. He was playing shite in the middle, especially when we didn't have the ball. Instantly it worked. Jeff flicked a ball on for Wardle who scored. We were on the up. Dunston eventually scored his solitary goal, which was a cracker and Wardle beat the keeper to slot in the fourth. They did manage to score another goal to make it 4-2, but the lad who scored came off the side-lines (injured or taking a drink – who knows?) to poke in the consolation.

Good game, enjoyable outing.

WHITE SHORTS WHITE SOCKS

Fines owed - 26th September 2004

Many of our players received letters from Dunsford League requesting payment for around £38. I informed them all that this wasn't official. Durham FA were trying to arrange a meeting with me and the TW League to sort out what we owed. The figure is £224 which equates to around £16-20 each. The process is straightforward. TW League will ask for a payment, the players refuse, and they will take the matter to Durham FA, who will arrange a meeting with me and TW League to decide on the amount we owed.

But typically, thick twat Wardle paid his straightaway. Moron. Next time I'm gonna send him a letter requested £20 toward my gas bill – he'd probably pay up as well. Greenwell also paid his, but his new manager paid his for him – must be desperate. That's the biggest problem with local football. We've got managers who probably had no mates at school and were crap at

WHITE SHORTS WHITE SOCKS

football so they get together a decent team where all the best players don't pay subs and then the manager might get a pat on the back in pub by someone saying he's got a decent team.

Defeating a poor league, off the pitch - 12th October 2004

Well, what can I say? This was D-Day. It was down to DFA to decide if we owed the Dunce League

£438 or the lesser amount of around £250. I was adamant that I would not being paying their fines. Question is – how the hell can you charge and entrance fee and an exit fee at the same time? Baffles me, but I suppose it's the norm for the Dunsford League. Their biggest problem is that people like me stand up to them and will do until my very last breath escapes me. And the reason why? Because I know exactly how to run a league.

I don't need a committee I just put plans into action and am always fair on my teams. The big meeting went ahead at the Dagmar as scheduled and despite the TW committee turning up with dossiers and dossiers of paper with their own "Weapons of Sassco destruction," they dithered over the exact timings of what they did and failed to show written evidence. Despite having four or five members of the committee there, it showed how unprofessional and badly organised the whole show is. One of many great moments was when John Topping,

DFA boss, asked the Dunsford League "who suspended Sassco from the League?" After several "hums" and

"errs" Jack Brown piped up and said, "It was you, John!" from which John Topping nearly choked.

Another point was the letter the Dunsford League sent to us saying we were going to be banned. They all said it was sent after the AGM on the 11th June. Topping pointed out that the date on the letter was 25th August! Laughable!

The key points which they failed on were as follows:

Failed to inform us in writing about the full amounts due.

Withheld our application to enter the following season and then said we resigned from the league.

Made the mistake by confusing the fact that Boothy resigned as Team Secretary, thinking the team had resigned.

Should have dealt with all cases within 21 days and not allowed the arrears to go on for so long.

Should NOT have sent letters to the players without letting DFA countersign them.

Did not take the disrepute about the messages on the website any further.

Claimed that J. Topping told them to suspend us.

The main objection the hearing had about Sassco was we shouldn't have not paid in the arrears and then stopped the cheque

Well, it's a valid point, but once I suspected that the TW League didn't want us in, I wasn't prepared to hand our arrears over (a large share of the £224 was due to be paid by me) and rather let the matter be dealt with each individual player who should pay their own share. Some of the lads won't be playing football this season (such as myself and Boothy, Galey, etc.) so it's down to the individuals to pay. Also, the fact that we were pulled up for disrepute meant if we handed £224 over, we could have been hit with more fines. The TW League simply didn't want us in.

In the end, we owed the League £264 which was paid immediately. All the lads also kept their part of the bargain and paid me around £18 each.

It was a huge triumph for me personally and concluded my business with the League (or so I thought).

The Police visit about a dodgy message - 14th November 2004

The long break did me some good. After an initial moping around stage on Saturdays, I eventually relaxed and enjoyed my weekends, especially the lie-ins. I also went on holiday. Two weeks in Florida at Disneyland was fantastic, but the on the second day back from the USA, I was readying to go to the Metro Centre when the cops knocked on my door. I knew exactly what it was about.

You see, the date when we got shafted by the Dunce League, was also the date when some arse put a classic message on the board. It wasn't me, but the comments were frighteningly harsh and possibly the most hilarious message I've ever read in my complete life. The person it was aimed at also read it and I always heard rumours that she was going to take some sort of action about it - and this was it.

WHITE SHORTS WHITE SOCKS

The coppers seemed a bit embarrassed, once they found out it was a message from an unknown and not directly from me as an editorial took a quick few scribbles and left. I didn't even get a slapped wrist and even had the nerve to tell them that I wouldn't take the message off unless the person complained to me directly to remove the message (which they didn't).

So that's around three or four times the Dunce's have tried to shaft us and failed.

…and they all lived happily ever after THE END

WHITE SHORTS WHITE SOCKS

It's 2024, 20 years later, and I'm still flogging a dead horse – September 2024

The diary ends in 2004, but Sassco has continued.

We did eventually join an afternoon league (Wearside Combination Football League – organised by my good friend, Peter Maguire – prominent in North East football) and remained there until the Summer of 2010, when I started the 2010-2011 season before quitting. A lot of my regular players had finished playing, so I decided to call it a day. An opening day 8-0 hammering also helped.

Since 2004, we've toured overseas in Malta and Portugal with the 11-a-side team in 2008 and 2009, with subsequent 5 or 6-a-side tours to Spain, Italy, Germany, France, Denmark, United States, Switzerland, Iceland, Israel, Cyprus. Holland after pandemic in 2023 and then a brilliant trip to Sweden in 2024 (with my son and

William Harper's son in tow). Only David Gourlay and I have been on every tour.

2024 was a great year in which we were invited to Scotland, Falkirk Stadium, to take part in an international tournament organised by Marc Boal – who is a contact from our Iceland tour. He'd arranged a number of tours for the Icelanders, so we were honoured to take part and even won the consolation trophy (wearing Admiral England 1982 type tops against a Scottish team in the final).

I've touched on racism and looking back at 2004 – twenty years ago, it seems quite interesting how life has changed for me and the attitude of first generation born here Asians.

For myself, I'm fully comfortable in my place in this country and society. When you get older, you give less shits. I'm now married to a white lady (since 2013) and society had changed, despite recent riots and issues. The day where I would be wary walking down any street has long gone and even the number of black and Asians now actually playing local football, going to matches, even playing for Sunderland is completely transformed.

The fabric of society had changed – yes, there are still issues, but if anyone says racism has gotten worse – they are a genuine fucking idiot.

WHITE SHORTS WHITE SOCKS

Back to the core of what this diary was about: The 11-a-side was resurrected in the Summer of 2011, when we had a couple of get-together friendly games and then this became a habit. In 2017, we re-joined an 11-aside league, albeit in 50-minute format and did the same again in the Summer of 2019.

We've also had three games at the Stadium of Light, as the regular team there, dropped down the divisions. We even played against the aforementioned Icelandic XI, who hosted us in Reykjavik a year before.

The 5/6-a-side get togethers are still going strong, as those are always easier to arrange and also formed the source of all the players, we called up for the 11-a-side. The Downhill Complex closed in 2015, and we were proud to hold a last hurrah there in 2015, as the regular

Tuesday league ended in 2011. However, it's re-opening in 2020 meant we gathered a set of teams for a tournament there in February and played bi-monthly (or thereabouts) for a few years. Prior to this, since 2015 it was a set of summer events in Washington Galleries, culminating in July 2019's tournament, with a few older heads from the past playing.

We've returned to Washington from summer 2023 and play every few months, with only a one or two players from the Sassco leagues taking part – including me, now aged 52, still doing around 1.5 miles on a 5-a-side pitch.

11-a-sides are few and far between. We played a few years back with three amazing summer games, all wins, against strong teams and ourselves being tactically astute, because players were shoehorned into the team having never played for the team before. In Summer 2023, we played and lost one game. This was the last set of 11-a-side games, but I'll end on a fascinating 11-a-side line up in an October 2018 game. We defeated a works team 11-2 and nearly half of the team who played in Sassco's first game back in 2001: Me, Gourlay, Dixon, Stubba and Muers, were there 17 years later for this one. To celebrate, Dixon now has special dispensation to wear his grey shorts instead of white. Grey because his lass put them in a mixed wash. Try a bit of white vinegar in the wash to brighten them up, Dixon. And don't step in any dog shit.

The End???

Davinder Sangha, September 2024

The following pages contain articles and messages gathered since 1999.

A random message on Sassco.co.uk message board - 2nd August 2003

This is a message which appeared on the message board Titled CARNAGE AT THE TURF, 2nd August 2003 and I just had to share the poetic genius. I suspect it was by Mr. John Hunt.

Recently, a high number of windows were mysteriously smashed in the vicinity of Downhill and upper Redhouse, Kestrel Square and Keverly Road were particularly hit hard when up to 13 motor vehicles were found to have cracked windscreens.

Police were called to the area at approximately 20.00 hours to investigate but after preliminary analysis by special ops and forensics, no evidence of malicious intent could be found. The busies were stumped.

At approximately 20.05 the massive clean-up

operation began to remove the mountains of broken glass from the streets, and it was at this time that a huge ear piercing shrill came from the direction of the Downhill 'turf....

As the noise built to a deafening crescendo, police dogs began to howl in a chorus of agonising despair, small animals emerged from the undergrowth and began running haphazardly into each other, police officers and residents sank to the knees clasping their heads as blood began to trickle from their ears and noses. The sound of shattering glass filled the skies as this 'sound from hell' began to rise in pitch and intensity...

Carnage was everywhere, old men crying, young women bleeding from every orifice (and i mean EVERY orifice), dogs and animals howling towards the heavens, teenage boys foaming at the mouth as the sound of glass shattering continued to reign from every direction...

A couple of off duty detectives, PC Tinge and DI Dink, who were busy munching McFlurrys at the local drive through, were quick to react and immediately stuffed the remnants of a discarded happy meal into their listeners and headed off toward the epicentre of the noise.

As they approached the 'turf, Tinge and Dink looked

toward each knowingly, with their happy meals lodged firmly in place they were completely oblivious to the rising noise, and as the they approached the pitch the scene, they saw would be burnt into their minds forever...

With a sound that could only be likened to a soprano opera singer hitting his highest note through a megaphone the size of a phone box, whilst simultaneously having his knackers clenched in a vice AFTER inhaling 8 gallons of industrial helium, Tinge and Dink soon realised everything. A game of six a side had been taking place but only now there were 2 players standing. The rest of the players were lying lifeless on the pitch, a grey sticky substance oozing from their ears. The referee was lying prostrate on the floor, eyes still bulging, mouth still agape, whistle still in hand as if he knew what was about to happen....

As Tinge and Dink scanned the area they saw that even the local posse of Dope fiends who congregated at pitch side were slumped in heaps across the bonnets of their second rate motors, shards of glass that used to be windscreens had lacerated them all, but one of them , later identified as 'Cheesy' was still sat perfectly upright, as if frozen in time, his features unchanged - blood shot eyes, stupid grin, ridiculous goatee, skins still being prepared in his grubby palms.....then suddenly the noise stopped, just like that - total silence.

Tinge and Dink approached the 2 players still looking at one another in the centre circle, oblivious to all around them, laughing in fact. As Tinge and Dink neared, they pulled out the happy meals from their listeners and reached for their holsters.... Tinge pulled out his 9mm Bumbag and pointed it at the first man, Dink pulled out his 12mm Man bag and pointed it at the second.

'Stop the pair of you! do not move or make a sound, if you do we will be forced to use physical force' 'You have the right to remain silent, you are hereby charged with multiple homicide, if found guilty you will face at least 30 years behind bars, be forced to sit in solitary confinement with Anth Langan for 30 days or if the judge is in a particularly bad mood, you could even be forced to sign on for Boldon Athletic for a whole season!'

It was at this moment that the first man, John Wardle, began to move toward DI Dink 'don't move Wardle, I wasn't kidding about Anth Langan' said Dink, but Wardle wasn't bothered, he knew their ears were unprotected now, and with no happy meals in sight Tinge and Dink were fucked. As Wardle began to sign

WHITE SHORTS WHITE SOCKS

Wuthering Heights by Kate Bush the second man, Steve Logan, made his move toward Tinge. 'listen Logan we can sort this out, hey, I can get rid of all those £5 fines you've incurred, I know people, you will never have to play with Mig again, I can do this for you!' but Logan was a machine, he didn't care, as he moved his head slowly from side to side , his neck bones cracking , he joined in with Wardle " ...it's me, its Kathy now come now, it's so cold...." and as the two of them reached the really high bit of the chorus, dark clouds raced overhead blotting out the setting sun, the sound of broken glass and howling dogs filled the skies once more and Tinge and Dink sank to their knees for the last time groping pathetically for a happy meal, their only hope of salvation that would never come.

Logan and Wardle, the greatest threat to mankind the world has ever known, genetic freaks blessed with unprecedented powers. . .who can stop them, maybe nobody, but what are we without hope?

WHITE SHORTS WHITE SOCKS

A Sunderland Earthquake, posted on 19th July 2003. Posted By: Redhouse Reporter

A major earthquake measuring 7.8 on the Richter scale hit Sunderland in the early hours of Friday 18th July 2003. The epicentre was Southwick Shops.

Casualties were seen wandering aimlessly saying "bang out of order", "mental" and "that did my head in". The earthquake decimated the area causing in excess of £17.55 worth of damage. Several priceless collections of mementos from Ibiza and Corfu were damaged beyond repair.

Three preserved areas of historic burnt-out cars were disturbed. Many locals were woken well before their giros arrived. The Echo reported that hundreds of residents were confused and bewildered. They are still trying to come to terms with the fact that the damage and destruction was caused by something else instead of them. One resident Tracey Sharon Smith, a 15-year-old

WHITE SHORTS WHITE SOCKS

mother of four said "it was such a shock, little Chardonnay-Leigh came running through the cardboard door into my bedroom crying. My young two, TylerBrooklyn and Kai-Keanu slept through it all. My hands were shaking so much I could hardly skin up when I was watching Trisha the next morning. Another local resident known as 'Mally' said that the earthquake would not stop him going to work, after all, the T.W.O.C'ing, burglaries and graffiti would not do themselves.

The British Red Cross has so far managed to ship 4,000 crates of Sunny Delight to the area to help with the crisis. Rescue workers are still searching through the rubble and have found large quantities of personal belongings, which include benefit books, jewellery from Jacky Whites, Bone China from Poundstretcher and several Argos catalogues. However, they were unable to save any furniture from Crazy Georges.

How can you help?

This appeal hopes to raise money for food and clothing parcels for those unfortunate enough to be caught up in the disaster. Clothing is most sought after. Most needed are Kappa or other tracksuits (his and hers), white socks to tuck the tracksuit bottoms into, Burberry caps, woolly 'Benny' hats and Reebok trainers.

WHITE SHORTS WHITE SOCKS

Primark clothing is

most welcome. Food parcels are also needed. They should include McCain's Micro-chips, Aldi beans, Monster Munch crisps, Nutella chocolate spread and Iceland pizzas. Alcohol is also in short supply, mainly Lambrini, White Lightning cider and Carlsberg Special Brew. Cash donations are also needed, 22p buys a Bic Biro for signing on purposes, £1.50 buys cheese and chips and £26 buys 200 Regal from 'Tommo' who has just got back from Kavos.

Wayne Greenwell: Being diagnosed and treated for Cancer – 13th February 2016

Written by Wayne Greenwell.

"Nothing is impossible, you just haven't done it yet. Dreams are hard to achieve, otherwise they wouldn't be a dream. In the darkest of hours when all seems hopeless, that's when dreams are made, more often than not in the face of adversity during those unsung hours. Never give up on those dreams as they inspire you to achieve what seems impossible."

Hi, let me introduce myself, my name is Wayne Greenwell, I'm 32 and I live in the City of Sunderland, England. I am writing this letter as an insight into how I felt and reacted whilst being diagnosed and treated with cancer in the great Freeman Hospital.

The Freeman really is second to none in expertise, care, and treatment in my opinion.

WHITE SHORTS WHITE SOCKS

In a way I want to strip back and expose my emotions that I had and still have to be honest when I was diagnosed back in June 2012.

I would also like to stress to you that I'm not an expert on cancer or an academic in this field or medically trained, but what I experienced and write about in this open letter may not be scientific, but it is my story, my feelings, my emotions that can't be forecasted no matter how advanced we are in medicine due to one simple fact, we are individuals within society and each to their own will react differently.

What follows in my words is factual and an honest account from me to you by ways of lessons learned and experiences as I underwent treatment not unlike possibly what you are now; I was or still am in the situation that you are facing and I hope that what follows helps you to get through what must feel like the darkest of times by knowing you are not alone.

Please imagine being in my shoes and see first-hand how I experienced and still am experiencing being a cancer patient; I would like to tell my story, even though just writing this is hard for me, because I am a man's man, I hope I come across as being totally open and transparent for the first time in my life when talking about how I feel.

WHITE SHORTS WHITE SOCKS

It's the height of summer 2012 and we are in the middle of a heat wave – yes, a heat wave in the UK! You have your whole life ahead of you as and then you get told you have "cancer" and it's "testicular". Not only do you have cancer but also, it's spread throughout your body to your bowels, lymph nodes', lungs, back and in three separate spots in my brain. Hearing this news, you might think that my whole world would cave in around me, well it never, in fact it had the opposite effect, and I would like to tell you why.

I had been unwell for a while; I first noticed blood in my semen the day before my 30th birthday and like a typical man I never thought much of it, it was a sort of ignorance that most men or people can relate to by having a sense of invincibility in the face of adversity during your youth. Nevertheless, I made an appointment that same day with my local GP and I honestly thought it would be something trivial like an infection or something along those lines as I sat in the waiting room.

I got called into the doctor's surgery, explained my condition and he said, "I think you've strained your testicle; I'm going to give you some anti-inflammatory tablets and then take some blood tests". I responded by telling him "I don't think I've strained my balls but ok", then I left the surgery with a prescription in my hand and went to the nurse's waiting room to have some bloods taken. Once I was called in and the needle was prepped, I asked, "so what are you checking me for?" To my surprise she said, "prostate cancer", I responded, "how do you know?", she said "it's the colour of the stickers for the tubes of blood, each colour is for a separate test".

Like I said, I was a little taken back by the news that it was cancer they were checking for as I thought this was a degenerate disease that took hold of older people, 60 plus etc… I thought nothing of it and went home that day as if nothing had happened.

Whilst I was younger, I was in and around cancer sufferers in my family. My gran, Jess and also my grandad developed cancer whilst I was in my early 20s; this exposure planted a mental block in my head when it came to be listening to the ambient awareness of the symptoms and understanding the disease. Some might say it's stupid, but I thought if you think about it, then it becomes a reality and it will get you. So, me being me, I pushed it aside in my mind and blocked out even saying the word.

My gran, Jess, developed women's cancer as I call it (or cervical cancer as the medical professionals' call it) and my grandad, unfortunately, developed it all over his body. This affected me in a big way because it scared me, and I don't scare easy because I'm British.

Just the exposure to the disease affected me when I was diagnosed, not straight away but when I was left alone to dwell on my thoughts, when my mind started running scenarios of what could be. This was a mistake and with hindsight I can reflect back now and say that, but in the moment, it consumed my confidence and optimism. I never showed it to those closest to me because I saw it as a weakness, I don't know if this was the right thing to do and I will never know what would have been if I had exposed my emotions to my loved ones. I stand by my decision and believe it was the right way, for me, to react; please don't use this as guidance as you will need to find your own unique persona to portray what makes you feel comfortable and mentally stronger.

If I could say this face-to-face, I would say "don't expect to be me, and think how I reacted but embrace your feelings and start from there, do your thing".

Don't listen to anyone else on how you should react, just be yourself and react in the way that your instincts tell you to. Don't waste emotional energy trying to be someone or something that you're not. Just accept that this is happening and do what feels natural to you as a person. Draw inspiration from around you but always be that person, "YOU ", always be you!

Before I was diagnosed, I hit rock bottom, this was because I went from an active outgoing person, to being restricted to a bed. I can tell you that I was diagnosed late, potentially too late for me. I remember my consultant telling me I had 2 days to live if I wasn't admitted to hospital and you know what, I was wishing it would be all over because of the pain I was in.

But with the diagnosis, I then realised what it was like to be alone, not alone in the sense of surroundings; my family and friends were there as you would expect, but alone in a battle against something that you can't see but only feel and I mean feel physically in terms of pain. I was in so much pain that I was ready to give up, ready to close my eyes and not wake again.

To be alive and looking forward to life, then wishing it was all over is a feeling I can only describe as being hollow and nothing but absolute desperation.

All I wished for was that the pain would go away, I was so fixated and unable to leave that moment due to the situation that dictated my life at that point, but and it's a big but in that moment of total hopelessness, I was consulted by my doctor on my situation and what the next steps would be to try and cure me. With this I was pleased, someone gave me a plan to start getting mended or fixed physically.

From that moment I had a different perspective on the situation and started changing my mindset thinking….

"Right my consultant (JF*) is giving me an option, I need to get inspired, come on Wayne this is not over yet "

I'm not saying it was an easy path I was forced down, but it did inspire me because another person had offered me an option to get better.

It was something to concentrate on and focus my mind; a sort of thing to look forward to and something to fight; a challenge to rise up to. Please take note; I was advised that I had little chance of being cured.

– And unbeknownst to me at the time, as I now reflect on my emotional responses that I had then, I still remember that I embraced this news and thought – "Right, let's see what is and what will be, I can beat this by not thinking about it and by getting on with my life outside this environment "

I'm not a person who likes floating through life as I enjoy challenges and trust me please, I'm not saying this as a cliché or using challenge as some buzz word from a book I have read, it's how I was feeling and still do. I challenge myself to understand my limits and to test my character when the chips are down. In my mind this is living – as pain and strain make the beer at the end of the challenge so much more enjoyable, ha ha.

I have climbed all of the peaks in the Lake District alone, I have done the 3 Peaks alone, I climbed Kilimanjaro in Africa (20,000 ft.) alone and I enjoy a physical challenge and don't mind being alone.

(You are starting to see a pattern, I'm a loner when it comes to a challenge, and looking back I was unsure why I always chose the option to do adverse challenges on my own. But reflecting now, I can say it's because I wanted to test myself, to understand my limit and to understand me).

Being alone makes you motivate yourself, to understand how you react when you don't want to go on anymore, when it's easier to give up.

In those dark hours, those unsung hours, you either draw on self-motivation and realize your dreams and goals or, you walk away and give up. Well I have never walked away from anything in my life and I wasn't about to start doing so now when I was diagnosed.

WHITE SHORTS WHITE SOCKS

Walking away for me was not an option, if it can be done, I will make it happen, maybe it's me being competitive, or maybe it's how we are all engineered but need to realize our opportunity.

We are born who we are and live our lives because of the decisions we all make. That decision-making process we make consciously, or sub consciously is what I think is human instinct. But that's just my opinion.

(We have no excuses neglecting the opportunity of life as humanity itself allows us to realize opportunities and inspires us to endless possibilities if we just dream)

If I'm honest I never really thought about my mindset at the time as my life was consumed.

(Maybe "consumed" is a hard word to use)

When I was diagnosed I was with my close friends and family, they were all passing on their sympathy at the time because I had cancer, I could see the horror and sorrow in their eyes and it made me upset, angry, vulnerable and feeling guilty for being poorly.

This at the time was not what I wanted, all I wanted was to be treated normally and ignore the reality of the position I was in.

To want this expression from those closest to me might seem strange from the outside, but it was everything I wished for, people expressing despair to me through body language and emotions, well it magnified the situation I was in and again, it scared me.

This expression of emotion gave reality to the situation and it did affect my mindset. To be without your ability to take on Cancer, as who you are, the added pressure or feeling like you are a victim and in a hopeless situation, well, it makes you more vulnerable to lose focus on who you are and to keep being positive when all else seems impossible. I think that is normal in the circumstances.

Being a Cancer sufferer, in my opinion, makes people reflect on their life, reminisce on lost opportunities, dream about what if and could have been if I did that instead ………

Well, I thought of nothing but wanting to get better, back to be who "I am", nothing more and nothing less, just to be me again and carry on my life as I was.

We all have our routines in life, our little ways and little wins that make us happy. They might not be to other people's liking or tastes, but the world would be a shadow of the place it is if everyone was generic. Society is what it is because it's made up with individuals and we all must express our individuality.

WHITE SHORTS WHITE SOCKS

I for one, when I was going through chemotherapy, tried to be the same person, I carried on doing what I had been doing before I was taken ill (within reason). I carried on with my life as normal as possible, some might say, I was not acknowledging the reality of the situation, but I disagree, I see it as not being defeated by the position I was put in.

I would like to express that I am human, I did have doubts on whether I would get through this illness and I also embraced the reality that I might not.

This realistic possibility can't be described in words.

It's a feeling that you have when dying throughout your body; it is a crippling emotion if you let it but like any emotion it can change if you want it to. If you knuckle down and fight it head on, let the tears flow, embrace the fact you still feel emotion. This is what I BELEIVE IS THE ESSENCE OF BEING ALIVE.

When I was released from hospital after a course of treatment, I tried to make more memories for those times that I needed them. When I was in hospital getting treated, I would use these memories to inspire me & help spur me on; to want and make more memories or moments, to look forward and not think about the here and now of reality. When I was getting treated in hospital, I was in for 5 nights every 21 days, 1 week of chemo that destroyed the cancer cells along with my Red and White cells. Every 2 weeks your Red and White cells naturally regenerate, so chemo was targeted after they regenerated for me in the 3rd week, hence every 14 days I had a new course of chemo that finished every 21 days, so a 3-week cycle.

I hated going into hospital even though it was saving my life, I had anxiety about being locked in hospital for a week. I never feared the place but had a strange feeling, it's hard to put into words, I hated being there but also wanted to be there. (Work that out yourself because I'm still confused).

The staff and nurses have a job to do like most of us in our normal lives, but the staff who worked on my ward in the Freeman, I believe went beyond the call of duty to make patients relaxed in the circumstance and feel at home.

Patients go through the trauma and emotion because its put on them, but the staff who care for those patients in good times and hard, well they are "extraordinary people working in extraordinary circumstances" and I for one will never forget the care, conversations, laughs, professionalism and compassion they showed me and the other patients.

To work in those conditions on a daily basis takes

WHITE SHORTS WHITE SOCKS

real courage and humanity. Thank you, all Ward 34.

As my treatment came to an end my tumour markers came down from a million to 164 after 6 cycles of chemo, not all the Cancer had gone but, it was a whole lot better than when I first got admitted. The night I was admitted I was rushed from Sunderland Hospital to the Freeman. I remember vaguely a nurse asking my name and I mumbled blllllarrrrrr. I also remember she asked the year and what sex I was. I said I don't know on both questions alarmingly ha-ha.

That's where my life changed. The next morning, when the morphine wore off, I had a strange feeling that others closest to me would find that me dying was harder than dying myself because of the emotional side effects.

Once I'm gone, I'm gone and those closest to me will have the pain of me gone and then live with the effects of the disease for the rest of their life.

This is a reality in my mind and my feelings that are not influenced by opinion; it is a description of my reality.

For me, I will always say and believe that Cancer affects the person with the disease physically, but that the individual's family deals with the disease and its effects for a lifetime.

I was thinking I would leave them with heartbreak and sorrow and sad times, I was upset with this and went into a shell, I became an emotional recluse so as not to upset those around me and put more pressure on their emotions.

(Please remember this is my account of events and my emotions at the time, this is not advised on what to actually do, you must decide what to do for yourself as that is what will help you, what I did helped me emotionally and that's all that counts given the circumstances).

After my 3rd – 4th – 5th and 6th cycle of Chemotherapy my tumour markers continued to fall, 160 to 60 – to 30 – to 15. All the way to < 1. When I was told there was no trace of Cancer in my blood tests, I reacted in a way you might think was strange from the outside, I felt nothing! No joy, no relief, no happiness. I was in a place I created mentally to protect myself from all emotion. Like I said earlier I was in a shell, a sort of state of emotionless animation. Reflecting back now I am pleased and excited that I have kicked Cancer in the ass, but I also don't let myself get too carried away in case it comes back. I do this in my head so I don't fall as far emotionally if diagnosed again, in a way I am making it more manageable to take a fall, this might be the wrong thing to do but who cares, it's my way of dealing with my diagnosis and it is working.

Nevertheless, I understand I am still suffering from retreating to my shell as I find it hard to be emotional. Maybe this new me is who I am, maybe I will again change if the circumstances so dictate in my life and I wouldn't want it any other way.

For the moment I am content with this reality, and I realise the situation I was in was life changing. It may or may not have changed me, but I am happy to know that tomorrow is a new day, and I might feel differently inside. "Live for the day" so to speak, this emotion and uncertainty is living in my opinion, being part of the unknown and not understanding your future.

Since my tumour markers hit <1, I have had one of my testicles removed and a cluster of lymph nodes in my abdomen taken out. The scars and effects will be with me for life, but they are who I am now and still to this day; I am insecure about the scars, they are big and ugly (A bit like me in a nutshell ha-ha). Another side effect from my operation is I can't ejaculate anymore.

For a man like me this was a huge knock in self confidence and self-esteem. Some people think I should be a wreck; Medical Professionals keep telling or insinuating I should be a wreck mentally and should/need to have help. I find this hard to understand, like I said earlier, each person is an individual and each to their own because we are not all the same and react differently, its instinctive the way we react in my opinion.

I won't deny I hit hard times, dark moments, but I never ever thought I couldn't deal with it myself. Instead, I looked at it as a challenge, to get better mentally/physically/emotionally. I will explain my process and how my mind worked as best I can in the following……

I was suffering (Mentally) to realise myself, to realise why we are here on earth, in existence. In my head I thought what the point in life itself is if this is all it has to offer (hurt, pain, suffering). I slipped deeper and deeper into my shell and hid my emotions so as not to let people see me weak, affected by my illness. I thought this was the manly thing to do at the time. I thought to myself, be strong and be a Man, stiff upper lip, good old English values.

I'm not sure if this was the right thing to do, but I never broke down, I never cried or worried about anything. I was emotionally dead to everyone and everything and this was the catalyst to my girlfriend and me splitting as I was an emotional recluse not capable of showing my true feelings.

The dilemma I have now is, "IS THIS THE NEW ME? ". I don't know who I am right now, but I want to find out and God willing I will have the time to do this.

Please do not take my experience and thought process as a way to react to your condition, react in your own way. Learn the lessons from my experience and use it to help your own battle. My only wish is to inform how I reacted in your situation, draw experience from my feelings as nobody can foresee what you will go through, but I hope this letter helps you prepare in your own way.

All I know is that I'm alive and I'm still able to make mistakes. At the end of the day, life is not living without the good times and the bad, they are what make us anticipate tomorrow and live in the moment of the emotions, we have to embrace every moment possible.

(Especially if you're like a Sunderland AFC fan, and me as moments of joy are hard to come by ha ha).

Thanks in advance for you reading my letter and I wish you all the best in your treatment. From my heart, please contact me if you want to talk, let your emotions rule you with someone who understands through experience what our feeling.

If needed, I will also meet you for a chat face to face, use my shoulder to lean on as I understand what you're going through. I'm at your disposal if needed and I would also like to offer an open invitation to the family and friends of Cancer fighters who would like to ask questions, or even just have a chat to help you stay strong so you can support your loved one.

Wayne Greenwell

As of 2024, he's long recovered and is now comfortably living life to the full with his girlfriend.

If you have read this book. I'd appreciate your comments on it and it's writing style. Comments to davinder.sangha@sassco.co.uk. Ongoing adventures of the team can be found at www.sassco.co.uk.

ABOUT THE AUTHOR

Born in Huddersfield in 1972.

Moved to Sunderland in 1985 (forced by parents)

Sunderland fan

Married – Divorced - Married

Three Children

One Granddaughter and One Cat

Printed in Great Britain
by Amazon